Debra Z. Basil, PhD
Walter Wymer, DBA
Editors

Social Marketing: Advances in Research and Theory

Social Marketing: Advances in Research and Theory has been co-published simultaneously as *Journal of Nonprofit & Public Sector Marketing*, Volume 17, Numbers 1/2 2007.

Pre-publication
REVIEWS,
COMMENTARIES,
EVALUATIONS . . .

"Timely. . . . One of the most VALUABLE contributions of the book is the set of papers that look specifically at how an organization adopts social marketing approaches and builds its future capacity to do so. Examples include the World Anti-Doping Agency concerned with a specific problem–doping in sports–as well as an agency focused on the public health system of the state of North Carolina. The examples illustrate what works and what is still missing in each environment and will provide readers interested in diffusing social marketing in the future with MANY VALUABLE INSIGHTS AND RECOMMENDATIONS FOR ACTION."

Alan R. Andreasen, PhD
McDonough School of Business,
Georgetown University

BEST BUSINESS BOOKS

Best Business Books®
An Imprint of The Haworth Press, Inc.

www.HaworthPress.com

Social Marketing: Advances in Research and Theory

Social Marketing: Advances in Research and Theory has been co-published simultaneously as *Journal of Nonprofit & Public Sector Marketing*, Volume 17, Numbers 1/2 2007.

Monographic Separates from the *Journal of Nonprofit & Public Sector Marketing*™

For additional information on these and other Haworth Press titles, including descriptions, tables of contents, reviews, and prices, use the QuickSearch catalog at http://www.HaworthPress.com.

Social Marketing: Advances in Research and Theory, edited by Debra Z. Basil, PhD, and Walter Wymer, DBA (Vol. 17, No. 1/2, 2007). *Examination into the adoption of various social marketing practices to positively impact behavior and better society.*

Current Issues in Political Marketing, edited by Walter W. Wymer, Jr., DBA, and Jennifer Lees-Marshment, PhD (Vol. 14, No. 1/2, 2005). *"AN EXCELLENT TEXT FOR A NUMBER OF UNDERGRADUATE AND GRADUATE CLASSES in both political science and marketing . . . . Addresses concerns across a wide variety of traditional academic disciplines but is also accessible to non-academics." Jonathan Knuckey, PhD, Associate Professor of Political Science, University of Central Florida*

Social Marketing, edited by Michael T. Ewing, PhD (Vol. 9, No. 4, 2001). *"Stimulating . . . Extremely timely . . . With contributions from eminent academics from diverse parts of the world, this book covers a wide range of ideas, research methods, and philosophical concepts." (Barry Howcroft, ACIB, MSc, BA, Professor of Retail Banking, Banking Centre, Longhborough University, United Kingdom)*

Marketing Communications for Local Nonprofit Organizations: Targets and Tools, edited by Donald R. Self, DBA, Walter W. Wymer, Jr., DBA, and Teri Kline Henley, MBA (Vol. 9, No. 1/2, 2001). *"Excellent . . . a test that is of great relevance to practitioners and academics alike. The authors have successfully produced a comprehensive review of the marketing needs of non-profit professionals/organizations and offer relevant sets of tools." (Ram Cnaan, PhD, Associate Professor, School of Social Work, University of Pennsylvania, Philadelphia)*

Volunteerism Marketing: New Vistas for Nonprofit and Public Sector Management, edited by Donald R. Self, DBA, and Walter W. Wymer, Jr., DBA (Vol. 6, No. 2/3, 1999). *"Offers the volunteer coordinator in these organizations the information needed to better understand where, and how, to effectively recruit and mobilize these increasingly important 'customers.'" (Michael J. Tullier, East Alabama Community Blood Bank, LifeSouth Community Blood Centers)*

Marketing University Outreach Programs, edited by Ralph S. Foster, Jr., BS, William I. Sauser, Jr., PhD, and Donald R. Self, DBA (Vol. 2, No. 2/3, 1995). *"Should be required reading . . . The authors not only know marketing but they also reflect a deep understanding of outreach and its place in the 21st century university." (James C. Vortruba, Vice Provost for University Outreach, Michigan State University)*

Public Mental Health Marketing: Developing a Consumer Attitude, edited by Donald R. Self, DBA (Vol. 1, No. 2/3, 1993). *"Provides a balance of theoretical and practical information on marketing local, state, and national mental health agencies." (Reference and Research Book News)*

Published by

Best Business Books®, 10 Alice Street, Binghamton, NY 13904-1580 USA

Best Business Books® is an imprint of The Haworth Press, Inc., 10 Alice Street, Binghamton, NY 13904-1580 USA.

Social Marketing: Advances in Research and Theory has been co-published simultaneously as *Journal of Nonprofit & Public Sector Marketing*, Volume 17, Numbers 1/2 2007.

The development, preparation, and publication of this work has been undertaken with great care. However, the publisher, employees, editors, and agents of The Haworth Press and all imprints of The Haworth Press, Inc., including The Haworth Medical Press® and Pharmaceutical Products Press®, are not responsible for any errors contained herein or for consequences that may ensue from use of materials or information contained in this work. With regard to case studies, identities and circumstances of individuals discussed herein have been changed to protect confidentiality. Any resemblance to actual persons, living or dead, is entirely coincidental.

The Haworth Press is committed to the dissemination of ideas and information according to the highest standards of intellectual freedom and the free exchange of ideas. Statements made and opinions expressed in this publication do not necessarily reflect the views of the Publisher, Directors, management, or staff of The Haworth Press, Inc., or an endorsement by them.

Library of Congress Cataloging-in-Publication Data

Social marketing : advances in research and theory / Debra Z. Basil, PhD Walter Wymer.
    p. cm.
    "Co-published simultaneously as Journal of nonprofit & public sector marketing, volume 17, numbers 1/2 2007."
    "Consists of articles resulting from the inaugural conference" Social Marketing Advances in Research and Theory" (SMART), held September 16-18, 2004 in Kananaskis, Alberta Canada [and] . . . sponsored by the Centre for Socially Responsible Marketing at the University of Lethbridge, Canada, in conjunction with the Society for Consumer Psychology"–P.
    Includes bibliographical references and index.
    ISBN-13: 978-0-7890-2965-2 (hard cover)
    1. Social marketing–Study and teaching–Congresses. 2. Social marketing–Congresses.
    I. Basil, Debra Z. II. Wymer, Walter W.
    HF5414.S635 2007
    658.8–dc22
                                                     2006038323

Social Marketing: Advances in Research and Theory

Debra Z. Basil, PhD
Walter Wymer, DBA
Editors

Social Marketing: Advances in Research and Theory has been co-published simultaneously as *Journal of Nonprofit & Public Sector Marketing*, Volume 17, Numbers 1/2 2007.

Best Business Books®
An Imprint of The Haworth Press, Inc.

www.HaworthPress.com

The HAWORTH PRESS Inc.

Abstracting, Indexing & Outward Linking

PRINT *and* ELECTRONIC BOOKS & JOURNALS

This section provides you with a list of major indexing & abstracting services and other tools for bibliographic access. That is to say, each service began covering this periodical during the the year noted in the right column. Most Websites which are listed below have indicated that they will either post, disseminate, compile, archive, cite or alert their own Website users with research-based content from this work. (This list is as current as the copyright date of this publication.)

Abstracting, Website/Indexing Coverage . . . . Year When Coverage Began

- *(IBR) International Bibliography of Book Reviews on the Humanities and Social Sciences (Thomson)*
  <http://www.saur.de> 2006

- *(IBZ) International Bibliography of Periodical Literature on the Humanities and Social Sciences (Thomson)*
  <http://www.saur.de> 1995

- ***ABI/INFORM Complete (ProQuest CSA)***
  <http://www.proquest.com> 2001

- ***ABI/INFORM Global (ProQuest CSA)***
  <http://www.proquest.com> 2001

- ***ABI/INFORM Research (ProQuest CSA)***
  <http://www.proquest.com> 2001

- ***Academic Search Premier (EBSCO)***
  <http://search.ebscohost.com> 2006

- ***Business Source Complete (EBSCO)***
  <http://search.ebscohost.com> 2006

- ***Business Source Premier (EBSCO)***
  <http://search.ebscohost.com> 2000

- ***MasterFILE Premier (EBSCO)***
  <http://search.ebscohost.com> 2007

(continued)

(continued)

Bibliographic Access

- ***Cabell's Directory of Publishing Opportunities in Marketing*** *<http://www.cabells.com/>*

- ***MediaFinder*** *<http://www.mediafinder.com/>*

- ***Ulrich's Periodicals Directory: International Periodicals Information Since 1932*** *<http://www.Bowkerlink.com>*

Special Bibliographic Notes related to special journal issues (separates) and indexing/abstracting:

- indexing/abstracting services in this list will also cover material in any "separate" that is co-published simultaneously with Haworth's special thematic journal issue or DocuSerial. Indexing/abstracting usually covers material at the article/chapter level.
- monographic co-editions are intended for either non-subscribers or libraries which intend to purchase a second copy for their circulating collections.
- monographic co-editions are reported to all jobbers/wholesalers/approval plans. The source journal is listed as the "series" to assist the prevention of duplicate purchasing in the same manner utilized for books-in-series.
- to facilitate user/access services all indexing/abstracting services are encouraged to utilize the co-indexing entry note indicated at the bottom of the first page of each article/chapter/contribution.
- this is intended to assist a library user of any reference tool (whether print, electronic, online, or CD-ROM) to locate the monographic version if the library has purchased this version but not a subscription to the source journal.
- individual articles/chapters in any Haworth publication are also available through The Haworth Document Delivery Service (HDDS).

As part of Haworth's continuing committment to better serve our library patrons, we are proud to be working with the following electronic services:

AGGREGATOR SERVICES

EBSCOhost

Ingenta

J-Gate

Minerva

OCLC FirstSearch

Oxmill

SwetsWise

FirstSearch

Oxmill Publishing

SwetsWise

LINK RESOLVER SERVICES

1Cate (Openly Informatics)

CrossRef

Gold Rush (Coalliance)

LinkOut (PubMed)

LINKplus (Atypon)

LinkSolver (Ovid)

LinkSource with A-to-Z (EBSCO)

Resource Linker (Ulrich)

SerialsSolutions (ProQuest)

SFX (Ex Libris)

Sirsi Resolver (SirsiDynix)

Tour (TDnet)

Vlink (Extensity, *formerly Geac*)

WebBridge (Innovative Interfaces)

Social Marketing: Advances in Research and Theory

CONTENTS

QUALITATIVE ARTICLE

CONCEPTUAL FRAMEWORK ARTICLE

ABOUT THE EDITORS

Debra Z. Basil, PhD, is an Associate Professor in the Faculty of Management at the University of Lethbridge. She has a PhD from the University of Colorado and a BA from the University of Washington. In addition she has seven years experience with a Fortune 500 company in various locations throughout the U.S.

Dr. Basil's research focuses on topics relating to charitable donations and corporate social responsibility. Specifically her research includes an examination of the process through which charitable guilt appeals generate donations, consumer response to cause-related marketing, consumer processing of nutrition labels, the impact of corporate support for employee volunteerism, and the use of social marketing in workplace safety campaigns.

She has published her work in the *Journal of Business Research,* the *Journal of Consumer Psychology, Psychology and Marketing*, the *Journal of Nonprofit & Public Sector Marketing*, the *International Journal of Nonprofit & Voluntary Sector Marketing*, and the *Journal of Health Communications*. She has received research grants from the Knowledge Development Centre/Imagine Canada as well as WorkSafe BC.

She is a founding member and former director of the Centre for Socially Responsible Marketing at the U of L. The CSRM creates and disseminates research in the area of social marketing, nonprofit marketing and corporate social responsibility. The CSRM hosts both academic and practitioner conferences, drawing participants from around the world.

Walter Wymer, DBA, is Associate Professor of Marketing at the University of Lethbridge in Alberta, Canada. He is a member of the University's Centre for Socially Responsible Marketing. He received his doctorate in marketing from Indiana University in 1996, then served as an Assistant Professor of Marketing at Jacksonville, later working at Christopher Newport University for nine years.

Dr. Wymer is Editor of the *Journal of Nonprofit & Public Sector Marketing* and North American Editor of the *International Journal of Nonprofit & Voluntary Sector Marketing*. He also serves on the editorial board of *Health Marketing Quarterly* and the *International Review of Public and Nonprofit Marketing*.

Dr. Wymer has focused his research efforts in various areas of nonprofit marketing for the past decade. He has published over 30 articles in scholarly journals and published in the proceedings of over 20 academic conferences. He has a text on nonprofit marketing which was published in 2006.

Foreword

This special issue consists of articles resulting from the inaugural conference "Social Marketing Advances in Research and Theory" (SMART), held September 16-18, 2004 in Kananaskis, Alberta Canada. The conference was sponsored by the Centre for Socially Responsible Marketing at the University of Lethbridge, Canada, in conjunction with the Society for Consumer Psychology.

SMART was an intimate conference that brought together academics and practitioners from around the globe to present their original social marketing research. Over 50 participants from seven countries were in attendance. The purpose of the conference was to provide an opportunity for researchers to share their work in a peer-reviewed, competitive paper format. This resulted in many high quality articles published here.

As both a practice and a field of academic study, social marketing is a process tool. Philip Kotler and his colleagues have been instrumental in this evolutionary process. One of the first definitions of social marketing was put forward by Kotler and Zaltman (1971):

> Social marketing is the design, implementation and control of programs calculated to influence the acceptability of social ideas and involving considerations of product planning, pricing, communication, distribution, and marketing research.

Later Kotler and Roberto (1989) modified this definition:

> a program planning process that promotes the voluntary behavior of target audiences by offering benefits they want, reducing barriers they are concerned about, and using persuasion to motivate their participation in program activity.

[Haworth co-indexing entry note]: "Foreword." Basil, Debra Z. Co-published simultaneously in *Journal of Nonprofit & Public Sector Marketing* (Best Business Books, an imprint of The Haworth Press, Inc.) Vol. 17, No. 1/2, 2007, pp. xxi-xxv; and: *Social Marketing: Advances in Research and Theory* (ed: Debra Z. Basil and Walter Wymer) Best Business Books, an imprint of The Haworth Press, 2007, pp. xvii-xxi. Single or multiple copies of this article are available for a fee from The Haworth Document Delivery Service [1-800-HAWORTH, 9:00 a.m. - 5:00 p.m. (EST). E-mail address: docdelivery@haworthpress.com].

Available online at http://jnpsm.haworthpress.com
xvii

This revised definition demonstrates an important refocusing. First, the addition of voluntary behaviour change is significant. Second, the managerial focus emphasized by the four P's in the earlier definition was replaced by a consumer-centric orientation, emphasizing benefits and barriers. Finally, Kotler, Roberto and Lee (2002) simplified the definition further:

> Social marketing is the use of marketing principles and techniques to influence a target audience to voluntarily accept, reject, modify, or abandon a behavior for the benefit of individuals, groups, or society as a whole.

This most recent definition has pared the issue down to its central essence–using marketing to encourage voluntary behaviour change for the good of individuals and society.

As Andreasen (2002) notes, social marketing has grown significantly since its introduction, both as an academic field of study and as a behavior change practice. In assessing the "maturity" of the field, social marketing appears to be in the growth stage (Rogers, 1995).

A search of Proquest's ABI/Inform Global article database seeking the term "social marketing" revealed 229 articles.[1] The first of these was published in 1971. In the seventies and eighties, just under four articles per year on average were published on social marketing. This number nearly doubled in the nineties, to just under nine articles per year on average. Since 2000, increase was apparent, evidenced by the publication of over 13 social marketing articles per year on average. Social marketing continues to grow in both application and sophistication.

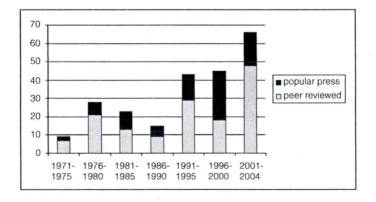

Initially, roughly three-quarters of the published articles on social marketing were academic. Social marketing then enjoyed greater exposure in the popular press in the eighties and nineties, with nearly 50% of the published social marketing articles coming from outside of academe. Since 2000, 73% of the published social marketing articles from this literature search originated in academe. This does not represent a decline in popular press interest, but rather the continued increase in academic interest.

Social marketing, both study and practice, has grown and evolved dramatically since its introduction by Kotler and Levy in 1969 (Andreasen, 2002). The convergence of a definition of social marketing, as well as the growing research interest in social marketing, suggest a field that has matured from a fledgling concept on the periphery to a valued and respected topic in its own right. Further evidence of this maturation can be seen in the emergence of seminal works within social marketing. This emergence suggests the adoption of a common core, where researchers collectively acknowledge what are the most central contributions to the field of social marketing. The articles within this special issue, as well as many recently published social marketing articles, reflect this paradigmatic development. These seminal works include (but are not limited to) social marketing books by Andreasen (1995), Rothschild's (1999), and Kotler, Roberto, and Lee (2002). For the SMART conference, and for this special issue, these pieces appear to have had a tremendous impact on the field. These works have served to unify our focus within social marketing. They represent seminal works that both bind and guide our efforts. More importantly, their emergence signals a level of sophistication within the field commonly enjoyed by mainstream lines of research.

The articles in this special issue seek to advance our understanding and use of social marketing through a variety of methods. The first of these methods is the case study approach. Three articles employ a case study approach to gain insight into the adoption of social marketing practices. The article by O'Reilly and Madill outlines the use of social marketing by the World Anti-Doping Agency. Madill and Abele then take a longer-term perspective with a case study of the Canadian Heritage Anti-Racism campaign, assessing the use of social marketing practices across the campaign's 12 year life. Finally, Newton-Ward applies a case study approach to North Carolina's Division of Public Health in an effort to assess their success in increasing the use of social marketing throughout their programs.

The second research method used is an experimental approach. Two articles adopted an experimental approach. Diaz Meneses and Beerli Palacio use a quasi-experiment to increase recycling. De Meyrick conducts an experiment to assess the validity of using on-line surveys for social marketing data collection with an adolescent population.

The third research method adopted was a qualitative approach. McGovern assesses the ability of social marketing to address transportation issues using qualitative data collection.

Finally, Peloza and Hassay develop a conceptual framework of charity support behaviors. This article represents the second track of research at the SMART conference, which addressed non-profit issues. As such it relates to the application of social marketing into the domain of influencing charitable behavior.

We believe the success of the SMART conference demonstrates the growing importance of social marketing as an academic field of study as well as a practice. The increasing number of social marketing publications, the emergence of seminal works, and participation in social marketing events such as SMART all demonstrate that the field is growing and maturing. Social marketing appears to have advanced to the mainstream of marketing study and practice.

Debra Z. Basil

NOTE

1. This search undoubtedly did not reveal all social marketing publications, as it was limited to one database.

REFERENCES

Andreasen, Alan R (1995), *Marketing Social Change: Changing Behavior to Promote Health, Social Development and the Environment*, Jossey-Bass Publishers, San Francisco.

_____ (2002), "Marketing Social Marketing in the Social Change Marketplace," *Journal of Public Policy and Marketing*, 21 (1), 3-13.

Kotler, Philip and Eduardo Roberto (1989), *Social Marketing Strategies for Changing Public Behavior*, The Free Press, New York, USA.

Kotler, P., E. Roberto, and N. Lee, (2002), *Social Marketing: Improving the Quality of Life*, Second Ed, Thousand Oaks: Sage Publications.

Kotler, Philip and Gerald Zaltman (1971), "Social Marketing: An Approach to Planned Social Change," *Journal of Marketing*, 35, 3-12.

Rogers, E. M. (1995) Diffusion of Innovations (4th Ed.). New York: Free Press.

Rothschild, Michael L. (1999), "Carrots, Sticks, and Promises: A Conceptual Framework for the Management of Public Health and Social Issue Behaviors," *Journal of Marketing*, 63 (October), 24-37.

CASE STUDIES

The World Anti-Doping Agency:
The Role of Social Marketing

Norm O'Reilly
Judith Madill

SUMMARY. Doping in sport poses a clear threat to the significant social and economic roles that sport plays in the world. To combat this threat, sport organizations and governments from around the world founded the World Anti-Doping Agency (WADA) to eradicate doping from sport. This article reports on research that documents and assesses approaches to anti-doping behavior utilized since early in the twentieth

Norm O'Reilly is Assistant Professor, Marketing, Faculty of Business, Ryerson University, 285 Victoria Street, Toronto, Ontario, Canada, M5B 1W1 (E-mail: noreilly@ ryerson.ca).

Judith Madill is Associate Professor, Marketing, Eric Sprott School of Business, Carleton University, 1125 Colonel By Drive, Ottawa, Ontario, Canada, K1S 5B6.

The authors would like to thank Richard Pound, President and CEO of the World Anti-Doping Agency, for both his time and support in carrying out this research. The authors would also like to thank two anonymous reviewers for their very valuable comments that helped the authors improve the article significantly. Any errors or omissions, of course, remain the responsibility of the authors.

[Haworth co-indexing entry note]: "The World Anti-Doping Agency: The Role of Social Marketing." O'Reilly, Norm, and Judith Madill. Co-published simultaneously in *Journal of Nonprofit & Public Sector Marketing* (Best Business Books, an imprint of The Haworth Press, Inc.) Vol. 17, No. 1/2, 2007, pp. 1-26; and: *Social Marketing: Advances in Research and Theory* (eds: Debra Z. Basil and Walter Wymer) Best Business Books, an imprint of The Haworth Press, Inc., 2007, pp. 1-26. Single or multiple copies of this article are available for a fee from The Haworth Document Delivery Service [1-800-HAWORTH, 9:00 a.m. - 5:00 p.m. (EST). E-mail address: docdelivery@haworthpress.com].

century including those used by WADA to achieve its goal of eradicating doping in sport. In particular, it assesses the extent to which social marketing is used in its strategy. Results show that sanctions and education are the major approaches employed to combat doping and that social marketing has not been used. Findings suggest that social marketing strategies, as a complement to WADA's current legal and education approaches, have a future role; demonstrating that, in a broader context, social marketing could enhance educational and legal approaches to behavior change. doi:10.1300/J054v17n01_01 *[Article copies available for a fee from The Haworth Document Delivery Service: 1-800-HAWORTH. E-mail address: <docdelivery@haworthpress.com> Website: <http://www.HaworthPress.com> © 2007 by The Haworth Press, Inc. All rights reserved.]*

KEYWORDS. Social marketing, sport marketing, international policy, not-for-profit marketing, anti-doping

INTRODUCTION

Sport plays an important social and economic role in virtually every country of the world. Examples of the global influence of sport range from the estimated 3.7 billion people from over 220 countries who watched in excess of 36 billion hours of television coverage of the 2000 Summer Olympic Games from Sydney, Australia (International Olympic Committee, 2000), to the 60.3% of men and 39.7% of women who attended sporting events in 2002 in Canada (Marketing Research Handbook, 2004), to estimates that 35 million people worldwide played at least one round of golf in 2000 (World Golf Foundation, 2003). At the national level, countries use sport to promote nationalism (Palmer, 2001) and there are endless examples of star athletes who influence millions of people as role models in their local markets (Shanklin and Miciak, 1996).

Sport currently faces an enormous threat from doping. In recognition of this threat, numerous sport organizations and governments from around the world founded and continue to support the World Anti-Doping Agency (WADA) and its mission to eradicate doping from sport. WADA defines doping as "the occurrence of one or more of the anti-doping rule violations" (WADA, 2003) as outlined in eight articles of its World Anti-Doping Code. These rules are broad, including "the presence of a prohibited substance or its metabolites or markers in an athlete's bodily specimen" (WADA, 2003), "tampering, or attempting to tamper, with any part of doping control" (WADA, 2003), and "administration or attempted administration of a prohibited substance or prohibited method to any athlete, or assisting, encouraging, aiding, abetting, covering up or any other type of complicity involving an anti-doping rule violation or attempted violation" (WADA, 2003).

In its short history, WADA has furthered anti-doping in sport. It has acted as the glue between governments and sport federations, bringing the majority of these organizations onside in the fight against doping (WADA, 2004b). It has attracted significant resources and funding (WADA, 2004d). It has brought profile to the cause as demonstrated by the inclusion of an anti-steroid message in President George W. Bush's State of the Union address to the United States Congress in January 2004 (Pound, 2004a). Further, WADA has played a role in bringing anti-doping to the forefront of some of the world's most suspected candidates for doping abuse, including the Tour de France bicycling race, and track and field in the United States (Deacon, 2004). In these respects and others, WADA is a very successful organization, however, in order to achieve its mandate, the organization must overcome significant barriers because of the complex social change relating to anti-doping that it must achieve in a number of stakeholder groups.

The marketing literature has shown consistent interest in social marketing, and recent attention has focused on the need to clearly define social marketing and expand its areas of application. Andreasen (2002) proposes a branding campaign that seeks to increase social marketing's share of the social-change market at the intervention, subject matter, product, and brand levels. It is the intervention level that is the focus of this article, where "social marketing can succeed by increasing the proportion of interventions that emphasize individual change (social marketing's niche) over approaches that emphasize community mobilization or structural change" (Andreasen, 2002). The purpose of this article is to report on research that:

a. presents a background overview of doping behaviors, as well as anti-doping approaches, utilized throughout most of the twentieth century within the context of a discussion on the structure of high-performance sport;

b. presents an overview of WADA and the approaches used by WADA to achieve its goal of eradicating doping in sport. In particular, it assesses the extent to which WADA uses social marketing;

   c. postulates a potential rationale as to why social marketing is not currently used in the WADA strategy. This considers the wide range of barriers identified in previous literature including a failure on the part of social marketers in building awareness of their field; and

   d. examines the present conditions at WADA and explores how social marketing could be integrated into the WADA strategy. In particular, the article provides, in the context of Rothschild's (1999) work, a broader and more generalizable explanation of what social marketing could add to educational and legal approaches for influencing athletes' use of doping substances.

Although WADA the organization could be described as "unique," it is an important organization that plays a critical role on the world stage by tackling a key problem in sport–doping. While focusing on WADA itself is important, a demonstration of the importance of social marketing as a means of social change will provide knowledge and support for the idea that other organizations acting at the intervention level can successfully adopt social marketing interventions as part of their strategy. The rationale for undertaking this study is derived from the important role that WADA plays in an important industry and the potential impact of social marketing both in that context and broader application.

Reflecting the major objectives for the article, it is organized into seven major sections. First, relevant background literature on social marketing is briefly reviewed. Next, the methodology used in the research is considered. Third, we provide a detailed background on the structure of high-performance sport, as well as an overview of doping behaviors and anti-doping approaches used to combat doping. The article then moves to an analysis of WADA, its development, organizational structure, funding, and the current approaches to achieving its goals. The extent to which social marketing is used and the barriers to its adoption are the focus of the next sections. We then discuss the potential of social marketing at WADA and how social marketing can contribute to furthering WADA's policy goals and objectives. Of particular importance in this section is an assessment of Rothschild's MOA theory (1999) in assessing generally how social marketing can complement educational and legal approaches to behavior change. Finally, the article's major findings are summarized and conclusions are presented.

BACKGROUND LITERATURE: SOCIAL MARKETING

It has been suggested that social marketing is a useful tool by which to develop and implement strategies and tactics toward changing behaviors (Andreasen and Kotler, 2003; Kotler and Roberto, 1989). In practice, social marketers work to encourage individuals or groups to adopt behaviors that are socially desirable (Andreasen, 1995). Previously, Andreasen, (1994) clarified that "influencing behavior is social marketing's fundamental objective." Social marketing is a relatively new agent of social/ behavior change that resulted from the Kotler and Levy (1969a, 1969b) proposal that marketing principles and tactics could be applied beyond their traditional boundaries to the marketing of services, persons, and ideas. A two-sided debate involving multiple theorists followed in the literature with the side that argued for expanding marketing's boundaries eventually winning over the side that argued for guarding marketing's traditional application in buy-and-sell transactions. Following Kotler and Levy's (1969a) suggestion that "marketing is a pervasive societal activity that goes considerably beyond the selling of toothpaste, soap, and steel" and asking "whether the principles of 'good' marketing in traditional product areas are transferable to the marketing of services, persons, and ideas," the debate began. One group of writers argues for the expansion of the concept of marketing (Kotler and Levy, 1969b; Kotler and Zaltman, 1971; Lazer, 1969; Shapiro, 1973) while another group (Bartels, 1974; Hutton, 2001; Luck, 1969, 1974) questions the long-term affects of applying marketing concepts to broader contexts, inferring that the definition of marketing should include only buy-and-sell transactions. Within the debate, a number of significant theoretical contributions were made. Kotler and Zaltman (1971) provided examples of churches, museums, and symphonies using marketing to increase membership, and charities using marketing to raise money. Kotler (1972) crafted a generic and very broad concept of marketing. Shapiro (1973) demonstrated how marketing theory could be applied to non-government nonprofit organizations. Bagozzi (1974) proposes marketing as a behavioral system of exchange, which established the basis for the future development of social marketing theory.

By the late 1970s, the application of marketing tactics to areas other than the private sector had increased dramatically, identifying the importance of considering strategies and tactics in addition to those traditionally employed (Rothschild, 1979). The rationale for this shift was to account for the complex differences between sectors (Laczniak, Lusch, and Murphy, 1979). In this context, social marketing developed rapidly in the practitioner and applied research (DeJong, 1989) settings driven by the increased need of nonbusiness organizations for marketing services.

Recently, research has pointed out some of the antecedents that allow for social marketing to occur. These include (among others): (a) open competition for the acceptance of ideas and behaviors that exist in developed countries (Rothschild, 2001), (b) increasing pressures on policy makers to implement their policies, and (c) increasing mobility in society with its accompanying decrease in the strength of traditional group norms influencing individual behaviors (Ouchi, 1980).

Defining social marketing and determining where it fits among the many subdisciplines of marketing has been a challenge for the field (Andreasen and Kotler, 2003). McMahon (2001) positions social marketing as "part of a larger, non-private market sector marketing concern which includes public-sector marketing, government marketing, political marketing, not-for-profit marketing, non-government-organization (NGO) marketing, charitable marketing, cause-related marketing, and voluntary or third-sector marketing." There is general support for the current definition articulated by the Social Marketing Institute (2003), defining social marketing as "the planning and implementation of programs designed to bring about social change using concepts from commercial marketing," although other theorists support similar yet subtly different definitions. Andreasen and Kotler (2003) stress that social marketing benefits the target audience and society in general, not the marketer. Brenkert (2001) clarified that when defining social marketing, one must consider that it is defined by its twofold nature: "its aim and the method it adopts to achieve that aim." Rothschild (2001) supports a definition that includes the dual objective of encouraging behavior change in the target audience and supporting the development of a related environment that is conducive to that change.

Recent advancements in the field include the development of the MOA (motivation, opportunity, ability) conceptual framework to manage social change (Rothschild, 1999) and the consideration of a relationship-based approach to social marketing (Hastings, 2003). Although applying the relationship paradigm advanced knowledge in the field, it was the development of the MOA implementation framework for behavior change that legitimized social marketing as one of the key intervention strategies of social change, along with educational and legal approaches. This relates to doping where each of education, law, and marketing are strategy choices available to WADA to encourage behavior change in athletes and their support teams.

The Adoption of a Social Marketing Approach

In practice, social marketing continues to struggle to grow as an approach to social change (Andreasen, 2002). Although many barriers to adoption have been identified in the literature (Andreasen, 2002; Rothschild, 1999), social marketing has been adopted and has been successful in a wide variety of circumstances and situations (Andreasen and Kotler, 2003). In many of these instances of success, social marketing has been used as an approach to complement education and the law as part of a comprehensive program of behavior change at the intervention level encouraging individual change (Andreasen, 2002).

A brief review of the anti-smoking literature illustrates how a social marketing approach can be effectively combined with laws prohibiting smoking and reveals a number of best practices that might be appropriate for use in anti-doping by an organization such as WADA. For example, a social marketing program must be evaluated and there are a variety of research methodologies by which to do so (Pechmann and Ratneshwar, 1994; Schar and Gutierrez, 2001). Further, 18 months to two years are required before an anti-smoking behavior change program will show significant results (Schar and Gutierrez, 2001). Pechmann and Ratneshwar's (1994) work argues for a comprehensive approach to behavior change, including education, marketing, and the law. The literature indicates that gender differences and ideologies must be considered (Rugkasa et al., 2003), that the media plays a powerful role in effecting behavior change (Keller and Brown, 2002), and that program evaluation needs to be considered in the program development stage (Dwyer et al., 2003). O'Connell et al. (2003) propose that a one-size-fits-all approach to behavior change is why many behavior-change programs are failing, suggesting that social marketing practitioners need to consider behavior-change programs based on segmentation and "impediment profiling."

Barriers to Social Marketing

The literature to date has considered the barriers to the adoption of social marketing programs, helping to determine situations where social marketing could be applied to overcome these barriers. Two of social marketing's most preeminent researchers (Andreasen, 2002; Rothschild, 1999) have identified eight key barriers to the adoption of social marketing strategies as outlined in Table 1.

TABLE 1. Barriers to the Adoption of Social Marketing

#	Barrier	Source	Description
1	Reliance on education and the law as approaches to social change	Rothschild, 1999	Need to show relevance of social marketing as a complement to education and the law
2	There is a difficulty in distinguishing social marketing from education	Rothschild, 1999	Education can suggest an exchange but cannot deliver the benefit of the exchange explicitly. Targets must figure out how to meet their own needs
3	Managers lack formal marketing training	Rothschild, 1999	Lack an appreciation for the self-interest of the client, the benefits of an exchange, and an understanding of power and competition
4	The ethics of social marketing	Rothschild, 1999	Trade-off between the rights and responsibilities of the individual and the society
5	There is a lack of appreciation of social marketing at top management levels	Andreasen, 2002	Research has shown acceptance of social marketing primarily at the practitioner level
6	The field has poor "brand positioning" and some perceive it as manipulative and not community-based	Andreasen, 2002	Fuzzy image, no clear definition, and no differentiation from other approaches to change
7	There is a lack of formally documented and publicized successes	Andreasen, 2002	There is a need to demonstrate the effectiveness of social marketing, superior to its alternatives
8	Social marketing lacks academic structure	Andreasen, 2002	There is a lack of courses, programs, faculties, and journals

(***adapted from Rothschild, 1999, and Andreasen, 2002)

METHODOLOGY

This article is a case study aimed at understanding approaches used to eradicate doping in sport, focusing particularly on the current and potential roles of social marketing for WADA as an approach to changing the behavior of athletes and support-team members who are doping. The choice of a case-study methodology to examine the application of a specific marketing program has precedence in the sport-marketing literature. Lachowetz and Irwin (2002) use a case analysis of a major corporate sponsorship of a charity golf event to demonstrate that a cause-related marketing program should be considered as part of an organization's overall marketing program. Generally speaking, a case-study approach is beneficial when the learnings can be applied to larger audiences. For example, Stauss and Friege (1999) use a case study to make the argument that a key opportunity for firms to increase or maintain their customer base is through the mining and evaluation of their database of defected customers.

The case study utilized data from two major sources. The first source was WADA documents including policies, programs, financial statements, and press releases. Many of these documents are publicly available from WADA's website (http://www.wada-ama.org). Twenty-four documents ranging from transcripts of speeches by the President of WADA to the 2004-2009 Strategic Plan were examined in the study. The analysis of these documents provided the background data for the second major data source, two in-depth interviews with the President and CEO of WADA, Richard Pound. The first interview took place on March 16, 2004 in Montreal, Canada. This interview lasted 60 minutes, was taped (with permission), then transcribed and analyzed for this article. The interview involved a prepared list of 23 questions developed from the background literature, followed by a general discussion. The second interview lasted 75 minutes and took place on April 7, 2004 in Toronto, Canada, and involved an extensive review of a first draft of this research, with the interviewer taking detailed notes.

DOPING AND ANTI-DOPING BEHAVIORS IN THE CONTEXT OF HIGH PERFORMANCE SPORT

Analysis of social marketing at WADA requires analysis of doping and anti-doping within the context of the world of high-performance sport. The next two subsections of this article contribute to the first major objective of this article by focusing on this analysis.

Doping, Anti-Doping, and Sport

Improving performance is inherent in the nature of competitive sport. Throughout the history of sport, athletes, trainers, and coaches have applied various methods toward improving athletic performance. Some approaches have been legal (i.e., nutrition, training practices, coaching, equipment improvements) while others have been illegal (i.e., drug-use, blood doping, bribery). One of these aspects that has been deemed illegal and in need of sanction is doping, or the use of performance-enhancing substances and techniques. The movement to eliminate doping is known as "anti-doping" and it has required some element of control ever since

Thomas Hicks won gold in the 1904 Olympic marathon with the help of a dozen raw eggs, injections of strychnine, and doses of brandy administered to him during the race (WADA, 2004a). Pre-1945, doping was primarily seen in the form of stimulants. Steroid use began in the late 1940s and was widespread by the 1960s (Pound, 2004b). Blood doping in various forms, in particular erythroproetin (EPO), began in the 1970s. Most recently, the performance-enhancing designer drug tetrahydrogestrinone (THG) is receiving attention (Wendt, 2004).

The first major organization to ban the use of performance-enhancing substances was the International Amateur Athletic Federation (IAAF) in 1928. Various other organizations followed suit but since no testing took place, the effectiveness of these bans is doubtful (WADA, 2004a). Pressure mounted in favor of testing as a result of new advancements in doping products and the deaths of athletes in competition due to drugs and, in 1966, the international federations for cycling and football were the first to introduce doping tests at their respective World Championships. The International Olympic Committee (IOC) followed suit in 1967 with the creation of its Medical Commission, which published its first list of prohibited substances shortly thereafter. Formal drug testing began at the Olympic Games (summer and winter) of 1968. The 1970s saw doping take center stage in the sport world due to the widespread use of anabolic steroids and the suspicion of state-sponsored doping practices (WADA, 2004a). The 1980s and 1990s saw a few high-profile positive doping results and more federations began testing. Testing procedures improved, and an "evident connection between more effective test methods and a remarkable drop in the level of top results in some sports in the 1990s" (WADA, 2004a) were demonstrated. In fact, at the 2000 Olympic Games, no world records or Top 20 all-time results were recorded in the athletics competition (Pound, 2004b). The evolution of widespread testing identified the additional challenge of developing positive tests that are legally supportable.

Background on High-Performance Sport

Sport, as an industry, is not homogeneous and this is particularly important from an anti-doping perspective. There is team sport and individual sport, professional sport and Olympic sport, high performance, development and participation sport, strength sport, and skill sport. For the purpose of this analysis, we consider the segment of sport that is most likely to be impacted by doping; namely the high-performance stream of sport. "High performance" refers to sport where performance is the principal goal (i.e., Olympic Games, professional sport), as opposed to development or participation. This stream is not limited to just elite international athletes; it includes any athlete who is on the track to high performance. This aspect of the high-performance stream reaching down to those not yet at the international level was supported by the CEO interview: "... it [the high-performance stream] obviously includes the international athletes and the entourage of those international athletes. Then, it reaches certainly down to the national level because that is where all these folks are coming from" (Pound, 2004a). In practical terms, the stream includes varsity athletes, national-level athletes, development-level athletes, and participation-level athletes in high-performance training environments with the objective of achieving performance success (i.e., junior national athletes). An important point is the consideration of the athlete's entourage (e.g., coach, trainer, family, doctor, masseuse) as part of the equation. In responding to a question about whether WADA is currently reaching athletes at the entry point of the high-performance stream, the following response was provided by the CEO: "I hope so, but we are going to have to start with and eat this particular elephant one bite at a time. You start at the international and get down to the national. What you hope is that there is a forced-down or trickle-down to the entry level. Certainly choices will have to be made with testing those people and whether you can rely on a 12- or 14-year-old to make that kind of decision [to dope or not] is hard to tell. You have to educate them, from something as broad as the public to educating the parents. Your child is not your way out of the ghetto, it's not your way to realize your own dreams in some vicarious manner, and coaches and legislators and educators all have to know that" (Pound, 2004a). These comments underline how far WADA's programs must reach and the fact that they must target an athlete and his or her entourage. In addition, they also emphasize the focus on education as a key strategy for WADA, one that the organization has been implementing effectively.

WADA: STRUCTURE, FUNDING, AND CURRENT STRATEGY

In 1998, the world's most celebrated cycling race, the Tour de France, was rocked by a scandal involving drug use. The negative publicity targeted all of sport, not just cycling, and in response, the IOC organized the inaugural World Conference on Doping in Sport in Lausanne, Switzerland, in February 1999. One of the proposed recommendations stemming from the conference–articulated in the Lausanne Declaration on Doping in Sport (IOC, 1999)–was to establish an independent international agency to apply global standards and coordinate the work of sport organizations and governments in support of anti-doping. On November 10, 1999, WADA was established as an independent, non-governmental organization with a mission "to promote and coordinate, at the international level, the fight against doping in all its forms" (WADA, 2002a). WADA was formed as a private foundation under Swiss law, with a somewhat unique structure based on equal representation of the Olympic Movement and Public Authorities (Howman, 2003), with a funding model of 50% provided by the Olympic Movement and 50% provided by various governments around the world (Pound, 2004b). Its business activities include conducting unannounced out-of-competition doping control among elite athletes, funding scientific research to develop new detection methods, observing the doping-control and results- management programs of major events, and providing anti-doping education to athletes, coaches, and administrators (WADA, 2004e). WADA has a physical presence in four cities: headquarters in Montreal, Canada, and regional offices in Lausanne, Switzerland, Tokyo, Japan, and Cape Town, South Africa.

WADA (2004c) is composed of a foundation board, an executive committee, and several working committees. The foundation board sets policy and the executive committee implements that policy and both are composed equally of government and Olympic sport representatives. WADA also has six working committees: Ethics and Education, Finance and Administration, Health, Medical and Research, Legal, and Standards and Harmonization (WADA, 2004c). WADA works through National Olympic Committees, government authorities, and National Anti-Doping Organizations (NADOs) to administer its programs. In terms of funding, WADA's, 2004 budget is based on $21,438,000 (US dollars); of which $10.1 million comes from the Olympic movement, $10.1 from public authorities, as well as $1.2 million from other sources (WADA, 2004d). The approved breakdown of government's contributions by region is outlined in the Cape Town Declaration (2001). Prior to 2002, the IOC funded WADA's start-up with a $25 million (US dollar) commitment over two years.

Given its role, resources, and government support, WADA is an important organization at two levels. First, in a broad sense, its success impacts society through its promotion of sport as clean and fair and the portrayal of its top athletes as role models to emulate. Second, WADA's success provides a level playing field where athletes can compete, train, and perform without questioning whether their competitors are cheating.

WADA and the World-Anti Doping Code

WADA's raison d'être is to eradicate doping from sport. It must be recognized that this involves changing behaviors at many levels in over 200 nation-states and dozens of sports. Understanding the various layers of stakeholders, interests, cultural differences, and political realities, WADA sought to develop a common, global policy that would ensure a level playing field across nations and cultures. The policy is the World Anti-Doping Code. Harmon (2003) pointed out that the Code has the "aim of harmonizing the multi-varied rules and laws then in effect around the world, and ensuring, in particular, that athletes are treated in the same manner by sports and governments in anti-doping issues." Following a detailed and consultative development process, the Code was adopted unanimously at the March 2003 World Conference on Anti-Doping in Copenhagen. Ninety-eight governments, 90 of 104 international sport federations and 178 of 202 National Olympic Committees have formally adopted the code as of February 2004 and it is WADA's objective to implement the Code at the 2004 Olympic Summer Games in Athens, Greece, and the 2006 Winter Olympic Games in Turin, Italy (WADA, 2004b). The IOC Charter was amended in 2003 and governments are developing an international treaty, through the United Nations Educational, Scientific and Cultural Organization (UNESCO), with the objective of ratification in October 2005 (Harmon, 2003).

An analysis of the World Anti-Doping Code reveals that its tenets are strongly rooted in, primarily, the law and, secondarily, education as ways to effect behavior change. The World Anti-Doping Code as published is comprised of three parts, the Code, International Standards, and Models of Best Practice. The Code provides the universal base upon which anti-doping programs are developed, the International Standards provide the technical and operational principles upon which anti-doping is implemented, and the Models of Best Practice will provide knowledge sharing of the best ways by which to implement the code (WADA, 2003). The first part of the World Anti-Doping Code is doping control. This part comprises the majority of the policy (46 pages) and involves the rules, regulations, testing processes, proof of doping, sanctions, and reporting. It also involves the legal aspects of doping. The second part of the Code is Education and Research. This section is very short (two pages) and provides the policy position on both education programs (e.g., what they should involve, how they should be set up) and research initiatives. Part three of the Code outlines the roles and responsibilities of each stakeholder, including the involvement of governments. This section is six pages. The final part (five pages) of the Code outlines the responsibilities and consequences to any stakeholder upon acceptance of the Code, compliance with the Code, modification of the Code, and its interpretation. This section outlines such aspects as penalties for non-compliance to the Code, the process to amend the Code, and the official languages of the Code. The Code focuses on the legal aspects of behavior change, touches on the educational aspect, but does not consider marketing, the other major method by which to encourage or reduce behavior change.

Current Usage of Approaches to Behavior Change at WADA

As a nonprofit organization, WADA's overall objective is to maximize adoption of doping-free behavior as opposed to profit (Ansari, Siddarth, and Weinberg, 1996). Background literature suggests that organizations can adopt combinations of education, marketing, and the law to achieve the appropriate behavior change in target markets (Binney, Hall, and Shaw, 2002; Rothschild, 1999, 2001). The precise combination of the three approaches is determined by whether or not the target has the motivation, opportunity, and/or ability to make behavior change (Rothschild, 1999).

A review of WADA's structure demonstrates a strong emphasis on both legal and educational approaches to behavior change. Of its functional concentrations, two (science, and standards and harmonization) have mandates that are directly related to sanctions (legal rules and regulations) and one (education) is exclusively devoted to education. The additional three units (communications, legal/finance, and human resources and corporate services) provide, for the most part, administrative support functions. There is no division responsible for social marketing. In terms of the allocation of WADA's 44 staff, 29 are involved in management, administrative support, and the operation of the three regional offices. Twelve employees work with sanctions (law) and three work in education.

WADA's 2004 budget reveals that sanctions (law) and education are WADA's priority. The proposed 2004 budget is $17,304,220. Of that budget, $10,507,400 (or 61%) is allocated to administration, finance, salaries, regional offices and operations, including research. The remaining $6,796,820 (or 39%) is allocated to primarily (34%) sanctioning (law) initiatives and secondarily (5%) to educational pursuits. Should any additional revenues be ascertained in 2004, the budget also specifies that, of any additional funds, 70% goes to research, 15% to out-of-competition testing, and 15% to education (WADA, 2004d). Further, the budget indicates no direct or indirect allocation of funds to social marketing.

WADA's 2004-2009 strategic plan further demonstrates WADA's focus on the legal and education approaches to social change. The strategic plan contains five overriding strategies for the next five years. "To oversee, support, implement, and monitor compliance of the World Anti-Doping Code" (WADA, 2004e) is objective one. Aspects of this strategy include both education and legal approaches. Objective two is "to educate and inform signatories to the Code, governments, and athletes/support personnel about the dangers of and consequence of doping abuse," (WADA, 2004e) which is entirely an education approach. Objective three is "to lead, coordinate, and support effective world-class anti-doping research programmes" (WADA, 2004e) which associates primarily with a legal approach as it relates to improved testing and sanctions. Objective four is "to increase the capability of anti-doping organizations (ADOs) to implement anti-doping rules and programs to ensure compliance with the code" (WADA, 2004e) and objective five is "to achieve the financial viability and resources to enable WADA to implement this strategic plan" (WADA, 2004e). Although vital to WADA's success, objectives four and five do not relate directly to behavior change.

The in-depth CEO interview supported the analysis of WADA documents. When questioned about the use of social marketing in strategic-planning meetings and discussion, the CEO replied: "it was not discussed mainly because our initial priorities were to get organized, get our stakeholders comfortable with the fact that they had financial obligations as well as involvement obligations, putting together the World Anti-Doping Code, working out arrangements with International Federations for testing protocols, and so on. We were really pretty focused in the short to medium term; the enforcement and legal side was priority one, then education (Pound, 2004)." This clearly demonstrates that legal and education approaches have been the priority for WADA to date and explains that they were the necessary approach of the time, given the context. At the conclusion of the first interview and following a discussion about social marketing, the CEO was asked if social marketing would be considered as an approach to adopt in the future. He responded "definitely" (Pound, 2004). The reader might note that the interview comments by the CEO of WADA may appear to be contradictory. Mr. Pound is quoted first as saying that he hasn't the faintest idea what social marketing is, yet later says social marketing would definitely be considered in the future. Interpreting these seemingly inconsistent comments requires consideration of the interview context. Mr. Pound was asked early in the interview about his understanding of social marketing–at this point he stated that he had no idea what social marketing is. However, a fairly detailed discussion of social marketing occurred later in the first interview and following that discussion, he made the comment about adopting it in the future.

The analysis to date has primarily addressed the first and second objectives of this article by documenting approaches to doping and anti-doping in the world or high-performance sport, and by focusing on WADA and its approaches to anti-doping. The research reveals that social marketing has not played a role historically at WADA, with legal and education approaches to behavior change taking priority in the quest to eradicate doping from sport. This is supported by the CEO's view (Pound, 2004a) on what the key to achieving anti-doping in sport is: "[since] you are dealing with a subset of society, it is a combination of prevention and sanctions where the rules are broken." This stepwise approach to behavior change is what an organization like WADA may be expected to do, as clearly rules must be established and target markets need to be made aware of such rules and the consequences of their behavior prior to embarking on any effort to convince change.

The next sections of the article move to an examination of why social marketing is not currently used in WADA strategy and to an exploration of how social marketing could be integrated into WADA strategy.

SOCIAL MARKETING: BARRIERS TO USE AT WADA

As summarized in Table 1, the literature provides a list of eight possible barriers to the adoption of social marketing. These potential barriers were utilized in this research to explore why WADA has not adopted social marketing to complement its sanctions and education programs. In the in-depth interview, the CEO was asked questions related to each of these eight barriers. These results are outlined in Table 2.

These findings strongly support the literature. Of the eight barriers identified by Andreasen (2002) and Rothschild (1999), seven have had a role in limiting the consideration of social marketing as part of WADA's overall strategy to social change. Of particular note is the CEO's volunteered admission, early in the first interview, that he has no idea what social marketing is (Pound, 2004a). It was clear from the interview responses as well, that WADA management and staff would have difficulty differentiating between education and marketing approaches. The likely rationale (and an identified barrier to adoption) is the fact that

TABLE 2. Barriers to Social Marketing at WADA

#	Barrier	CEO Quote
1	Reliance on education and the law as approaches to social change	*Results of the analysis of WADA documents described previously support this
2	There is a difficulty in distinguishing social marketing from education	"Yes [we consider our education programs to be a form of social marketing], because they are designed to alter behavior and bring about certain outcomes"
3	Managers lacking formal marketing training	"Less than 10% [of WADA's directors and managers have formal marketing training]."
4	The ethics of social marketing	No related comment
5	Lack of top management appreciation of social marketing	"I haven't the faintest idea [what social marketing is]" (Pound, 2004)
6	Poor brand positioning of field	No related comment
7	There is a lack of formally documented and publicized successes	"IOC's marketing programs are essentially social marketing" (Pound, 2004), in response to question "Are you aware of any successful social marketing programs?"
8	Social marketing lacks academic structure	"Not as such but I don't often get into that level of curriculum" (Pound, 2004) when asked, "Are you aware of any universities that offer courses in social marketing?"

(***Barriers adapted from Rothschild, 1999, and Andreasen, 2002)

"less than 10%" (Pound, 2004a) of WADA senior management (or only one member of the management team) has had formal marketing training. Their expertise lies in law and education. Given this, it is unlikely that a social marketing approach would be a priority for WADA as it pursues its anti-doping goals and objectives.

The case study on WADA suggests that while social marketing has not been considered to date by the organization, there is a definite openness to considering it in the future. In fact, Pound (2004a) believes that social marketing has a role to play in the generation of resources: "we have to find a way to increase the funds we have and a lot of that will be in the social marketing area." Further, he outlined that both senior management and staff at WADA would be open to consider social marketing (Pound, 2004a). However, following some reflection, the CEO also questioned whether social marketing and sociology were being confused (Pound, 2004b), indicating continued uncertainty about the field, perhaps related to the field's inability to position its own brand (Andreasen, 2002).

In its five years of existence, WADA has experienced considerable growth in building awareness of its existence, acquiring stakeholder support, launching education programs, and developing anti-doping sanctions. It is an organization that is highly respected and considered successful. The CEO has performed very well, and recently the Board expressed confidence and support to have him continue as CEO for another term (WADA, 2004f).

THE POTENTIAL ROLE OF SOCIAL MARKETING IN WADA STRATEGY

Although social marketing has been absent at WADA, examples of opportunities for its adoption have recently begun to present themselves. Certainly, the process of convincing governments and sport organizations to adopt and implement the World Anti-Doping Code is a possible situation for social marketing. In addition, the Athlete Outreach program launched during the Salt Lake City Olympic Games and implemented again at both the Commonwealth and the Pan American Games (Pound, 2004a), is another strong example of a situation ideal for a social marketing approach. Consistent with Rothschild's position (1999, 2001), this case study suggests that a social marketing strategy offers the potential to complement educational and legal approaches to behavior change, both at WADA and for broader application. A number of potential roles for social marketing are presented here.

First, some doping athletes may experience "negative demand" where they may not see a problem with their doping behavior (Andreasen, 1995). Negative demand means that the doping athlete has no need or want for changing his/her behavior (i.e., an exchange, in marketing terms, will not take place). In such situations, marketing could be used to complement legal and education approaches to encourage the adoption of anti-doping behavior. On one side of the exchange, marketing could encourage a doping athlete to recognize the significant costs of their doping behavior. These costs might include potential health risks as well as the risks associated with a positive doping test. The damage that would follow from experiencing a positive doping test cannot be overstated, and may include the termination of one's career, the disgrace and loss of prestige and status, loss of potential and/current sponsors and government support. Further, in losing one's career or incurring a suspension, the athlete's concept of self is significantly altered and/or damaged. On the other side of the exchange, a marketing strategy would develop a program to enhance the benefits that could accrue to an athlete who engages in anti-doping behaviors. Benefits might include not experiencing a positive doping test and reducing health risks (presently and in the future). The marketing approach would require that marketing research be done to understand what drives an athlete to adopt an anti-doping approach (both the costs of doping and the benefits of anti-doping) as well as the best ways to reach this group. Such information would be used to design marketing strategy.

It is important to note that marketing would be used to complement the legal and education approaches currently being used by WADA. Akin to smoking, it is possible that a doping athlete may downplay the risks of doping to their health. Used in collaboration with education, a marketing approach would undertake marketing research to truly understand athletes' thinking concerning the risks and rewards they face, leading to strategy based on this understanding. Marketing, in conjunction with a legal approach, will ensure the athlete understands that all athletes who dope will get caught. This is a critical point because the athletes who engage in anti-doping behavior as well as those who currently dope need to be assured of a level playing field. Marketing can play an especially critical role in this context–education and legal approaches probably cannot succeed on their own.

Another contribution of adopting social marketing is that it will enhance or clarify thinking about the WADA *product*. A social marketing framework positions the WADA product as "anti-doping behavior." An important part of what athletes want in engaging in anti-doping behavior is a level playing field–the understanding that no competitors in any country or at any competitive level will be doping. Therefore, an effective testing procedure is necessary, making it part of the product of WADA.

The innovative tactics of a social marketing approach can offer considerable potential to WADA. In considering the competition to WADA's product (anti-doping behaviors), it must recognize at least two major competitors including both the alternate behavior (doping) and commercial marketing (fostering an environment where performance is highly valued). Innovative strategies to behavior change (that legal and educational approaches cannot offer) are required to compete effectively (Andreasen, 1995). For example, personal selling as a social marketing tactic to convince athletes to change to (or continue) doping-free behavior could be implemented by former top athletes following training in social marketing.

Andreasen and Kotler (2003) suggest three important dimensions in successfully changing social behavior. These include exchanges that are (a) high or low involvement, (b) onetime or continuing, and (c) by individuals or groups. Doping is clearly a high-involvement product (high risk, high cost, high level of self-expression) that involves such emotions as anxiety, guilt, and denial (Berkowitz et. al., 1999). Further, the decision to dope or not is continuous, as it is considered by an athlete from the day they enter high performance sport until they retire. Doping can be either an individual or group decision. Mr. Pound's (2004b) view is that the entourage or group around the athlete is particularly important in the doping decision. Therefore, according to Andreasen and Kotler (2003), doping will be a difficult behavior to change. In these situations, Kotler and Roberto (1989) suggest that a social marketing approach is particularly effective. However, WADA should be realistic in its timelines and expectations regarding social marketing.

Rothschild's MOA Framework: Learning from WADA

As noted, Rothschild's (1999) theoretical framework (see Figure 1) positions social marketing along with law and education as the strategic tools of behavior management and each is considered based on the target market and whether or not its members have the motivation, opportunity, and/or ability to potentially change their behavior. "Motivation" refers to the goal-directed arousal of targeted individuals, "opportunity" considers the openness of the environment to individual change,

FIGURE 1. Applications of Education, Marketing and Law

MOTIVATION	Yes		No	
OPPORTUNITY	Yes	No	Yes	No
ABILITY Yes	#1 prone to behave *education*	#2 unable to behave *marketing*	#3 resistant to behave *law*	#4 resistant to behave *marketing, law*
No	#5 unable to behave *education, marketing*	#6 unable to behave *education, marketing*	#7 resistant to behave *education, marketing*, law	#8 resistant to behave *education, marketing*, law

and "ability" represents the aptitude of the individual target to change or solve problems (Rothschild, 1999). The targets themselves are considered based on whether they are prone, resistant, or unable to comply with the policy maker's objectives. "Prior levels of motivation, opportunity, and ability in the target will determine behavior and will lead to a target being prone, resistant, or unable to behave" (Rothschild, 2001).

The framework supports the potential advantages available to WADA of adopting social marketing as part of a comprehensive program of behavior change. Of the eight scenarios outlined in the model, six include marketing as one of the recommended approaches to change and one of these scenarios involves marketing as the only choice of behavior change (Rothschild, 1999). In particular, Rothschild (1999) shows that marketing may be the only approach that can be used for behavior change when the target is motivated to change, has the opportunity to change but is unable to change. When one considers high-performance sport, this target defines many of the athletes who are doping. These are athletes who want to change and exist in an environment that provides the opportunity to change but are not able to change for a number of reasons (Pound, 2004a) including financial, political, and competitive (Pound, 2004b).

This analysis argues for the integration of a complementary social marketing strategy where education may not work because some athletes do not see that resisting doping is necessarily in their best interests. Such athletes need to see the positive benefits that could accrue to them if they adopt an anti-doping approach. A social marketing program could clearly lay out these benefits and highlight their attractiveness vis-à-vis the current doping behavior. In a series of questions relating to Rothschild's scenarios, WADA's CEO supported the MOA framework, admitting that, although these athletes are not currently being reached, "we will [reach them] in the future when we have a much more comprehensive program in place" (Pound, 2004a). As part of this comprehensive program, the CEO indicated that WADA is willing to consider social marketing (Pound, 2004b).

Results also provide evidence of the need for constructing the next iteration of the Rothschild model (1999). The case research points specifically to the need for a more detailed version of the MOA model specific to complex social marketing products such as anti-doping where motivation, opportunity, and ability are not binary *yes* or *no* constructs. Rather, as this case study illustrates, it is likely that conflicting and complicated motivations come into play. Taking Rothschild's model and the WADA athlete who is resistant to anti-doping behaviors as an example (Rothschild, 1999), block #4 in Figure 1 demonstrates that a more detailed consideration of each of motivation, opportunity, and ability is needed in future model development. For example, considering motivation, earlier discussion indicates a multitude of complex and conflicting factors on both sides of the exchange process that need to be considered as motivating the athlete. Similarly, when considering opportunity to change, the WADA case suggests athletes operate in widely varying national contexts (with differing levels of acceptance of doping practices across countries). This finding, in combination with recognition that a group frequently makes the anti-doping decision (e.g., coach, physician, athlete), points to the need to articulate a more detailed model that considers country, culture, and context under ability to change. Upon confirmation from future research, the case may provide the basis for further refinement and development of the Rothschild framework.

SUMMARY AND CONCLUSIONS

This article focused on four major objectives. First, it briefly described doping and anti-doping behaviors in the context of high-performance sport. It focused specifically on documenting the structure and strategies employed by WADA in pursuing its goal of eradicating doping in sport. In particular, the research examined the extent to which WADA uses social marketing. This research shows that to date WADA has extensively employed both legal sanctions (identifying and banning performance enhancing substances) and education programs as approaches to behavior change, while a review of documentation and interviews with the CEO revealed that a social marketing approach has not been considered. Public education was centered on informing athletes, coaches, and trainers about the doping behaviors and anti-doping measures to be employed. Examples include a WADA and International Paralympic Committee joint sanctioning and education program targeted at Paralympic athletes (The Paralympian Online, 2001) and the Australian Football League's anti-doping policy, which was limited to education programs about testing and penalties (Australian Football League, 1990).

In addressing the third objective of the article, the case study on WADA supports the existence at WADA of barriers to the adoption of social marketing (Andreasen, 2002; Rothschild, 1999). In particular, there is a lack of understanding of social marketing among senior management, as well as a lack of training in marketing in general at senior management levels. Overcoming these barriers will be essential if social marketing is to make its mark. This task falls in the purview of social marketing professionals who need to take a stronger role in marketing the benefits and roles for social marketing.

Finally, the article examined current conditions at WADA and explored how social marketing could be integrated into its strategy. In spite of the current non-use of social marketing and a lack of understanding of social marketing, the research shows that support for the use of social marketing exists within the organization at the highest levels (the CEO). This suggests that support for the idea of social marketing may exist in cases where little knowledge about it exists. The question raised is, "Why does this support exist?" Future research is required to focus on measuring attitudes toward social marketing among potential users of this approach in both government and not-for-profit organizations. Such research will assist and inform the efforts of those concerned with the marketing of social marketing in the future (Andreasen, 2002).

It was shown that barriers to the adoption of social marketing at WADA exist and that social marketing appears to offer much potential within this environment to contribute to social change. A number of potential social marketing strategies and tactics were identified. Although the risk of extrapolating findings from a single case study must be recognized, the results presented here support strongly that WADA could adopt social marketing as part of a comprehensive program of behavior change.

Within the context of Rothschild's (1999) work, the article offers a broader explanation of what social marketing could add to educational-legal approaches to behavior change. Future research is required to verify both assertions focusing on the adoption of the social marketing approach within a wide range of government and not-for-profit organizations. Future work is needed both generally in exploring social marketing's potential role in organizations in similar environments and specifically at WADA in developing social marketing plans and tactics that the organization could implement and adopt as part of its overall strategy. The research calls for the field to consider a new iteration of the Rothschild MOA framework specific to high involvement, continuous group decisions. Finally, follow-up research on WADA's attempts to adopt social marketing as part of its future strategy is a worthwhile project. Should such research determine that social marketing is successful at WADA, organizations acting as change agents in industries such as health, international trade, human rights, and the law could adopt similar social marketing approaches.

REFERENCES

Andreasen, Alan R. (1994), "Social Marketing: Its Definition and Domain," *Journal of Public Policy and Marketing, 13*(1), 108-14.

_____ (1995), *Marketing Social Change: Changing Behavior to Promote Health, Social Development and the Environment,* Jossey-Bass Publishers, San Francisco.

_____ (2002), "Marketing Social Marketing in the Social Change Marketplace," *Journal of Public Policy and Marketing, 21*(1), 3-13.

Andreasen, Alan and Philip Kotler (2003), *Strategic Marketing for Nonprofit Organizations,* 6th Edition, Prentice Hall, New Jersey, USA.

Ansari, Asim, S. Siddarth, and Charles B. Weinberg (1996), "Pricing a Bundle of Products or Services: The Case of Nonprofits," *Journal of Marketing Research,* 33 (February), 86-93.

Australian Football League (1990), *AFL Anti-Doping Policy,* www.afl.com.au; downloaded March 4, 2004.

Bagozzi, Richard P. (1974), "Marketing as an Organized Behavioral System of Exchange," *Journal of Marketing, 38,* 4 (October), 77-81.

Bartels, Robert (1974), "The identity crisis in marketing," *Journal of Marketing, 38* (October), 73-76.

Berkowitz, Eric, Frederick Crane, Roger Kerin, Steven Hartley, William Rudelius, and Debi Andrus (1999), *Marketing: Fourth Canadian Edition,* McGraw-Hill Ryerson, Toronto, Canada.

Binney, Wayne, John Hall, and Mike Shaw (2002), "A New Social Marketing Model: Testing and Application of the MOA Framework," *Journal of Social Marketing,* www.social-marketing.org.

Brenkert, George (2001), "The Ethics of International Social Marketing"; in *Ethics in Social Marketing,* ed. Alan Andreason, Georgetown University Press, Washington, USA, 39-69.

Deacon, James (2004), "Enemy of the Bad Guys," *Maclean's,* July 26, 2004, 39.

DeJong, William (1989), "Condom Promotion: The Need for a Social Marketing Program in America's Inner Cities," *American Journal of Health Promotion, 3*(4), 5-16.

Dwyer, John J.M., Barbara Hansen, Maru Barrera, Kenneth Allison, Sandra Ceolin-Celestini, Dan Koenig, Deborah Young, Margaret Good, and Tim Rees (2003), "Maximizing children's physical activity: an evaluability assessment to plan a community-based, multi-strategy approach in an ethno-racially and socio-economically diverse city," *Health Promotion International, 18*(3), 199-208.

Hastings, Gerard (2003), "Relational Paradigms in Social Marketing," *Journal of Macromarketing, 23*(1), 6-15.

Howman, David (2003), "Sanctions Under the World Anti-Doping Code," speech given to the World Anti-Doping Agency, November 12, 2003.

Hutton, John G. (2001), "Narrowing the Concept of Marketing," *Journal of Nonprofit and Public Sector Marketing, 9*(4), 5-24.

International Olympic Committee, (1999), *The Lausanne Declaration on Doping in Sport,* http://www.olympic.org.

_____ (2001), *Global TV Broadcast Sets Records for Sydney 2000 Olympic Games*," Lausanne, Switzerland.

Keller, Sarah N. and Jane D. Brown (2002), "Media Interventions to Promote Responsible Sexual Behavior," *Journal of Sex Research, 39*(1), 67-73.

Kotler, Philip (1972), "A Generic Concept of Marketing," *Journal of Marketing, 36* (April), 45-54.

Kotler, Philip and Sidney J. Levy (1969a), "Broadening the Concept of Marketing," *Journal of Marketing, 33*(1), 10-15.

_____ (1969b), "A New Form of Marketing Myopia: Rejoinder to Professor Luck," *Journal of Marketing, 33*(July), 55-57.

Kotler, Philip and Eduardo Roberto (1989), *Social Marketing Strategies for Changing Public Behavior*, The Free Press, New York, USA.

Kotler, Philip and Gerald Zaltman (1971), "Social Marketing: An Approach to Planned Social Change," *Journal of Marketing, 35*, 3-12.

Lachowetz, Tony and Richard Irwin (2002), "FedEx and the St. Jude Classic: An Application of a Cause-Related Marketing Program (CRMP)," *Sport Marketing Quarterly, 11*(2), 114-118.

Laczniak, Gene, Robert Lusch and Patrick Murphy (1979), "Social Marketing: Its Ethical Dimensions," *Journal of Marketing, 43*(Spring), 29-36.

Lazer, William (1969), "Marketing's Changing Social Relationships," *Journal of Marketing, 3*(January), 3-9.

Luck, David J. (1969), "Broadening the concept of marketing—too far," *Journal of Marketing, 33*(July), 53-55.

_____ (1974), "Social Marketing: Confusion Compounded," *Journal of Marketing, 38*(October), 70-72.

McMahon, L. (2001), "The Impact of Social Marketing on Social Engineering in Economic Restructuring," *Journal of Nonprofit and Public Sector Marketing, 9*(4), 75-84.

O'Connell, Meghan, Sean C. Lucan, Ming-Chin Yeh, Elaine Rodriguez, Dipti Shah, Wendy Chan, and David L. Katz (2003), "Impediment Profiling for Smoking Cessation: Results of a Pilot Study," *American Journal of Health Promotion, 17*(5), 300-303.

Ouchi, W. (1980), "Markets, Bureaucracies and Clans," *Administrative Sciences Quarterly, 25*(March), 129-41.

Palmer, Catherine (2001), "Outside the Imagined Community: Basque Terrorism, Political Activism, and the Tour de France," *Journal of the Sociology of Sport, 18*(2), 143-61.

Pechmann, Cornelia and Srinivasan Ratneshwar (1994), "The Effects of Antismoking and Cigarette Advertising on Adolescents' Perceptions of Peers who Smoke," *Journal of Consumer Research, 21*(1), 236-51.

Pound, Richard (2004a), In-depth CEO Interview, Montreal, Quebec, March 16, 2004.

_____ (2004b), In-depth CEO Interview, Toronto, Ontario, April 7, 2004.

Rothschild, Michael L. (1979), "Marketing Communications in Nonbusiness Situations or Why It's So Hard to Sell Brotherhood Like Soap," *Journal of Marketing, 43* (Spring), 11-20.

_____ (1999), "Carrots, Sticks, and Promises: A Conceptual Framework for the Management of Public Health and Social Issue Behaviors," *Journal of Marketing, 63*(October), 24-37.

_____ (2001), "Ethical Considerations in the Use of Marketing for the Management of Public Health and Social Issues"; in *Ethics in Social Marketing*, ed. Alan Andreasen, Georgetown University Press, Washington, USA, 17-38.

Rugkasa, Jorun, Barbara Stewart-Knox, Julie Sittlington, Pilar Santos Abaunza, and Margaret P. Treacy (2003), "Hard boys, attractive girls: expressions of gender in young people's conversations on smoking in Northern Ireland," *Health Promotion International, 18*(4), 307-314.

Schar, Elizabeth H., and Karen K. Gutierrez (2001), "Smoking Media Cessation Campaigns from Around the World: Recommendations from Lessons Learned," *Technical Report sponsored by the Centers for Disease Control and Prevention in collaboration with the World Health Organization*, June 2001.

Shanklin, William L. and Alan L. Miciak (1996). "Selecting sports personalities as celebrity endorsers," *Journal of Promotion Management, 4*(1), 1-11.

Shapiro, Benson (1973), "Marketing for Nonprofit Organizations," *Harvard Business Review*, September-October, 223-32.

Stauss, Bernd and Christian Friege (1999), "Regaining Service Customers," *Journal of Service Research, 1*(4), 347-61.

The European Union (2003), *The Aarhus Declaration on Voluntary Work in Sport*, http://europa.eu.int/.

The Paralympian Online (2001), *World Anti Doping Agency and IPC Agree to Groundbreaking Testing and Education Program*, www.paralympic.org.

The Social Marketing Institute (2003), *Definition*, www.social-marketing.org.

Wendt, John T. (2004), "The Continuing Impact Of and Challenges to the New World Anti-Doping Agency and World Anti-Doping Code," *North American Society for Sport Management Conference*, Atlanta, USA, June 4, 2004.

World Advertising Research Centre (2004), *The Canadian Marketing Handbook 2004*, Oxfordshire, UK.

World Anti-Doping Agency (2001), *The Cape Town Declaration on Anti-Doping in Sport*, International Intergovernmental Consultative Group on Anti-Doping in Sport, Cape Town, SA.

_____ (2002a), *The World Anti-Doping Agency Annual Report*, www.wada-ama.org.

_____ (2002b), *WADA Strategic Plan 2002*, www.wada-ama.org.

_____ (2003), *The World Anti-Doping Code,* www.wada-ama.org.

_____ (2004a), *A Brief History of Anti-Doping*, www.wada-ama.org.

_____ (2004b), *WADA Code Acceptance*, www.wada-ama.org.

_____ (2004c), *WADA Composition Report*, www.wada-ama.org.

_____ (2004d), *WADA 2004 Budget*, www.wada-ama.org.

_____ (2004e), *2004-2009 Strategic Plan*, http://www.wada-ama.org.

_____ (2004f), *WADA Board Report, June 21*, http://www.wada-ama.org.

World Golf Foundation (2004), *Industry Report*, http://www.golf2020.com.

doi:10.1300/J054v17n01_01

From Public Education to Social Marketing: The Evolution of the Canadian Heritage Anti-Racism Social Marketing Program

Judith Madill

Frances Abele

SUMMARY. Social marketing plays a critical role in a multitude of government programs, yet little research has examined how social marketing programs commence and develop over time. Utilizing a case-study methodology, this article documents the evolution of a large-scale social marketing program–the March 21 Canadian Heritage anti-racism campaign. The research reveals that this program did not begin as a social marketing program, but rather as a public-education campaign. Over the years it took on many, but not all, of the characteristics of a

Judith Madill is Associate Professor, Eric Sprott School of Business, Carleton University, 1125 Colonel By Drive, Ottawa, Canada, K1S 5B6 (E-mail: Judith_madill@carleton.ca).

Frances Abele is Associate Professor, School of Public Policy and Administration, Carleton University, 1125 Colonel By Drive, Ottawa, Canada, K1S 5B6 (E-mail: frances_abele@carleton.ca).

The authors would like to thank Joan Murphy for her important research support in carrying out this study. The authors would also like to thank two anonymous reviewers for their very valuable comments that have helped the authors improve the article significantly. Any errors or omissions, of course, remain the responsibility of the authors.

[Haworth co-indexing entry note]: "From Public Education to Social Marketing: The Evolution of the Canadian Heritage Anti-Racism Social Marketing Program." Madill, Judith, and Frances Abele. Co-published simultaneously in *Journal of Nonprofit & Public Sector Marketing* (Best Business Books, an imprint of The Haworth Press, Inc.) Vol. 17, No. 1/2, 2007, pp. 27-53; and: *Social Marketing: Advances in Research and Theory* (eds: Debra Z. Basil and Walter Wymer) Best Business Books, an imprint of The Haworth Press, Inc., 2007, pp. 27-53. Single or multiple copies of this article are available for a fee from The Haworth Document Delivery Service [1-800-HAWORTH, 9:00 a.m. - 5:00 p.m. (EST). E-mail address: docdelivery@haworthpress.com].

social marketing program. Further research expanding the scope of this study and examining whether this evolutionary pattern is common for government and not-for-profit social marketing programs at other levels, in other sectors, jurisdictions, and countries is recommended. The results are thought to be of interest to those concerned with both the theory and practice of developing strategies for the marketing of social marketing. doi:10.1300/J054v17n01_02 *[Article copies available for a fee from The Haworth Document Delivery Service: 1-800-HAWORTH. E-mail address: <docdelivery@haworthpress.com> Website: <http://www.HaworthPress. com> © 2007 by The Haworth Press, Inc. All rights reserved.]*

KEYWORDS. Social marketing, public education, case study, barriers, adoption, and innovation

INTRODUCTION

One of the most significant recent developments in nonprofit marketing is the increasing utilization of social marketing by government agencies and nonprofit organizations as they endeavour to change problematic social behaviors. There are a variety of approaches that can be utilized to reach the goal of behavior change (Kotler and Roberto, 1989; Maibach and Parrott, 1995; Rothschild, 1999) including education, social marketing, and the law, among others. The literature has suggested that the potential for social marketing is vast: education is most appropriately used when people are uninformed but will be motivated to make changes once they become knowledgeable; law is appropriate when people who are knowledgeable refuse to act on this knowledge; and social marketing is appropriate for all other cases (Rothschild, 1999).

While there is much agreement that social marketing is playing a critical role in a multitude of government programs, little research has examined how these social marketing programs come into existence and develop over time. It is commonly recognized that marketing is not part of the mind set and philosophy of employees in either government or nonprofit organizations–in fact, they may not understand marketing or they may be philosophically opposed to the utilization of marketing and see it in negative terms (Andreasen, 2002; Madill, 1999; Rothschild, 1999). Facing such barriers, it is important to try to document how social marketing might come to be a significant tool in government behavior-change programs.

The purpose of this article is to document the evolution of a large-scale Canadian social marketing program, the March 21 Campaign, Canadian Heritage's anti-racism campaign. The article utilizes an in-depth case study methodology in tracing the evolution of this program over a 12-year period from its inception until the turn of the millennium in 2000. The Canadian Heritage March 21 anti-racism program was set up in 1988 by the Canadian government to respond to the United Nations' International Day for the Elimination of Racial Discrimination. This International Day commemorates the 1960 massacre of peaceful anti-apartheid demonstrators in Sharpeville, South Africa. While many countries honor March 21 with anti-racism events and activities, Canada is apparently the only country in the world to have a permanent program with dedicated staff devoted to achieving anti-racism in commemoration of this day.

This research shows that this program did not begin as social marketing, but rather as a public-education campaign. Gradually, over the years, it began to take on the characteristics of a social marketing program until at the conclusion of the case study, one can see the major components (but not all components) of social marketing within the program. While this case research reveals this pattern of development, it is important to conduct further research to expand the scope of this study and examine whether this evolutionary pattern is common for government and not-for-profit social marketing programs at other levels, as well as in other sectors, jurisdictions, and countries. The research results are thought to be of interest to those concerned with the developing theory as well as strategies for the marketing of social marketing (e.g., Andreasen, 2003).

The next section of the article briefly outlines previous research on the adoption and development of social marketing programs. Diffusion of innovation theory is presented in support of the proposition guiding the current study. This literature review is followed by a description of the methodology employed in this case study. The major portion of the article traces and outlines the development of the Canadian Heritage anti-racism social marketing program from its inception through to the turn of the millennium in 2000. Finally, the article concludes with a summary and discussion of the key findings from the study and suggestions for future research.

BACKGROUND LITERATURE

What Is Social Marketing?

Current definitions of social marketing suggest that it seeks to influence social behaviors "not to benefit the marketer but to benefit the target audience and the general society. Social marketing programs, then, by definition are generic marketing programs carried out to change behaviors that are in the individual's or society's interests." (Andreasen and Kotler, 2003).

How Social Marketing Differs from Other Approaches to Behavior Change?

A variety of approaches to behavior change have been discussed in the literature. As far back as 15 years ago, Kotler and Roberto (1989) proposed five types of major change strategies: social marketing, technology, economics, politics and law, and education. Rothschild (1999) argues for three types of strategies including education, marketing, and the law. Andreasen (2002) suggests six types of alternative approaches to behavior change ranging from the stages of change approaches, social learning theory to strategic communications and enter-education programs. These authors agree that the role for marketers is to induce voluntary behavior change, as opposed to passing laws or rules that attempt to force people to act or merely educating people, hoping they will act.

Following Kotler and Roberto (1989) and Rothschild (1999), Andreasen (2002) argues that what makes social marketing potentially unique is that its major goal is behavior change. Following from that goal, he goes on to state that it is customer-driven and emphasizes the creation of exchanges that will encourage a behavior change on the part of the targeted market. Because of this customer orientation, social marketing programs will be characterized by consumer research, pretesting, and monitoring, careful market segmentation when appropriate, and strategies that seek to provide beneficial exchanges to target audience members. Andreasen (2002) proposes that the benchmarks for identifying an approach that could be legitimately called social marketing include the following:

- Behavior change is the goal.
- Projects consistently use audience research
- There is careful segmentation of target audiences

- The central element of any influence strategy is creating attractive and motivational exchanges with target audiences.
- The strategy attempts to use all four Ps of the traditional marketing mix; for example, it is not just advertising or communications.
- Careful attention is paid to the competition faced by the desired behavior.

Andreasen (2002) is quick to point out that programs do *not have to have all elements* in order to qualify for the label "social marketing." However, campaigns that are purely communications campaigns are not social marketing. Hastings (2003) proposes that just as relationships have become critical in developing strategy for generic and commercial forms of marketing, they are now a critical feature for social marketing. Given that partnerships have traditionally been important features of many social marketing programs, the importance of relationships in social marketing programs appears clear.

Factors Encouraging Use/Adoption of Social Marketing

Ouchi (1980) postulated that the more in concert a community is and the greater the existence of regular communication channels between members of that community, the more likely the members of that community will act in a like manner and respond similarly to education. It is with more individualistic societies that marketing can play a greater role (Rothschild, 2001). In today's society, it is expected that community bonds are weakening as people tend to go away from home to study and often settle somewhere other than their hometown. These societal trends suggest much potential for the role of social marketing in the future.

In keeping with these expectations for its considerable potential, social marketing has been applied in a wide variety of situations ranging from helping teens to resist smoking (McKenna, Gutierrez, and McCall, 2000; Pechmann and Reibling, 2000) to exercising regularly, eating a healthy diet, following speed limits, wearing a seat belt while driving, and donating organs (Lwin, Williams, and Lan, 2002). Although these applications and others provide evidence of the growth in use of social marketing and hint at the potential for its future growth, "...leaders of the field remain concerned lest the upward movement should plateau prematurely before social marketing's full potential is realized" (Andreasen, 2002, 3). So, while it must be stressed that the domain of potential applications of social marketing is very broad, "...at any point, the real potential domain is only where members of society will sanction its application" (Andreasen and Kotler 2003, 330).

Barriers to the Adoption of Social Marketing

A recent analysis by Andreasen (2002) summarizes four major barriers to the growth of social marketing. Topping this list is the lack of appreciation of social marketing at top management levels. Andreasen writes that while social marketing has achieved significant acceptance among practitioners at the operations level of many implementing organizations, senior managers and leaders of too many nonprofit organizations and major government agencies are unaware either of social marketing or of its potential for organizing and implementing major social change. Because of this lack of appreciation, promising potential campaigns often do not use social marketing approaches. A second barrier noted by Andreasen (2002) is that social marketing is perceived by key influential people as having several undesirable traits and is not adequately differentiated from its competition, especially in ways that would be in its favor. The third barrier is that social marketing is perceived to have attributes that are unattractive to important target audiences–most prominently the perception that social marketing is manipulative and not "community based." The latter is a trait that is particularly important to many agencies and foundations that are involved in international development.

DIFFUSION OF INNOVATION: THE THEORETICAL PERSPECTIVE

Both knowledge transfer theory (Szulanski, 1996, 2000) and diffusion of innovation theory (Rogers, 1962, 1983, 1995) show the difficulties of diffusing and transferring knowledge concerning complex technologies and innovations such as social marketing. Diffusion of innovation theory (Rogers, 1983, 1995) shows that five key dimensions of an innovation will slow its adoption by organizations: (1) high complexity, (2) low compatibility with current organization values and practices, (3) low observability, (4) low trialability, and (5) low perceived advantage of the new approach relative to current and previous practices. In applying this theory to the adoption of social marketing by government organizations, one can see that social marketing suffers from high complexity, low compatibility with government practices, few opportunities to observe social marketing in action in like organizations for like purposes, as well as few opportunities to try it out in one's organization. It has also been shown that social marketing may not be well understood by senior managers in not-for-profit and government organizations, so its relative advantages may not be perceived or well understood. Diffusion of innovation theory provides considerable theoretical support for the recognition and understanding of barriers of adopting social marketing within large government organizations.

SUMMARIZING THE CONTEXT AND GOAL FOR THE CURRENT ARTICLE

In summary, existing theory and research show that while the potential for social marketing is considerable, a number of barriers exist to the adoption of social marketing in situations where it might offer potential for influencing behavior change. The researchers propose that because of the existence of such barriers, social marketing programs often begin as something other than social marketing programs. It is expected that they may often begin as public-education programs because such programs do not suffer from these same barriers. Over time, social marketing programs evolve from such programs. This research explores this proposition by focusing on the development of the Canadian Heritage anti-racism program over a 12-year period.

METHODOLOGICAL APPROACH

In keeping with the major purpose of the research, to document the evolution of the Canadian Heritage March 21 anti-racism campaign, the case study was based primarily on a review of 38 internal and public documents (which are listed in the References with Canada as the major author–preceded by an * in the list for easy identification). This approach allowed the utilization of the most objective data possible that documented the characteristics and features of the program over the years since its inception and development from 1988-2000.

The majority of the documents included in the study had been publicly released and were available from the resource center in the unit. Annual reports back to 1997 are available from the Web site (http:// www.pch.gc.ca/progs/multi/reports/index_e.cfm). The publicly available documents included information kits about the March 21 Campaign, organizer kits, teacher guides, participants kits, public polling results used by the March 21 management team for strategy development, as well as annual reports. Other documents were not publicly released and were obtained from the management team and staff specifically to enable the research. These included strategic plans and evaluations of the program as well as external consultants' reports recommending strategic areas for program development.

While the written documentation served as an objective source of the characteristics of the program over time, it did not provide much explanation as to how and why social marketing concepts came to be introduced into the program, only that they did. To augment this analysis, three semi-structured interviews were conducted with the people who had, over the years, created the March 21 Campaign. This portion of the study included an interview with the Minister of State (Multiculturalism) responsible for the March 21 Campaign as well as with two senior public service managers who had been involved in managing the program over the years. The interviews were all conducted by members of the research team who approached each interview with a prepared list of semi-structured questions that focused on clarifying issues raised in the written document analysis as well as on the issues of how and why the program developed in the way that it did, and the public policy context of the program. The interviews were conducted during the spring and summer of 2000 and lasted between forty-five and ninety minutes each. Detailed notes were taken during each interview. As well, members of the research team attended three staff meetings over this time period as observers. Since it is well recognized that relying on respondents to recall the past is fraught with recall bias, the focus of the methodology was to document objective changes through the analysis of documents. However, because insights into how social marketing ideas came to be diffused among the managers and incorporated into the program was also of interest, some understanding of this was gained through the interviews. This goal was a secondary focus of the research.

Utilizing the literature on what is known about the characteristics of a social marketing program (Andreasen, 2002; Hastings, 2003), an analytical framework was developed to assess characteristics of the program over the years. The framework examined the extent to which each of the following elements were present in the program over the years:

1. The use of the 4 Ps

   • Product
   • Promotion

- Pricing
- Distribution channels

2. Extent of market segmentation and target marketing
3. Development and presence of a strategic plan to guide the program
4. Whether the program was set up to facilitate an explicit exchange
5. Evaluation–Was consumer research done to evaluate and were these findings used in future developments of the program?
6. Relationships–Did the program emphasize relationships and/or partnerships?

FINDINGS: THE EVOLUTION OF THE MARCH 21 CAMPAIGN FROM PUBLIC EDUCATION TO SOCIAL MARKETING

Analysis of the case documents showed that the program's evolution was characterized by two important phases or stages:

- Phase I: Getting Started: The Public Education Years, 1988-1993
- Phase II: The Shift From Public Education to Social Marketing, 1994-1999

Tables 1 and 2 summarize the basic elements of the March 21 Campaign in each of these stages as well as the extent to which the features of social marketing programs (outlined in the methodology) were found to characterize the program in that time period.

A number of key highlights emerge from the tables:

1. *Consistency and Change.* Insights gained from both the interviews and the staff meetings revealed that management and staff remained highly committed to the goals of eliminating racism in Canada and worked extremely hard to achieve this goal. While retaining a consistent commitment to promoting citizen action against racism, the March 21 Campaign has changed significantly over the years.
2. *Discernable Phases.* The March 21 Campaign began in 1989 as a relatively conventional public awareness program with minimal private-sector sponsorship. The program expanded its reach each year. In the mid-1990s it defied early expectations by expanding activities and adopting more social marketing tools, motivated largely by the straitened circumstances of a period of federal government cutbacks and program review (see section Diffusion of

TABLE 1. Phase 1–Getting Started 1988-1993

Product (Program Elements)	Promotion			Distribution Channels
	Messages	Media/Communication	Pricing	
Product Description A major emphasis on information kits, public-service announcements and posters and booklets. ***1988-89*** Booklets and posters suggesting activities • A creative writing contest on eliminating racism • Regional offices organizing displays and discussion groups • Speeches and interviews by Minister of Multiculturalism • Minister presented eight awards for Excellence in Race Relations • Billboards and transit posters ran in 8 cities • Televised public service announcement aired on 95 stations • Distribution of information kits to community groups, institutions and opinion leaders • 30 municipalities proclaimed March 21 and held special events	Messages not actionable–primarily were for education and information. Analysis showed inconsistencies in messages used via different media, i.e., broadcast messages were not always congruous with print campaign. Slogans and messages changed almost every year– little consistency over time.	Engaged an ad agency for professional communications Information Kits sent to schools across country Posters distributed: – schools – government agencies – departments various partners Media campaign included radio and television broadcast messages	Assessment of written materials and interviews indicated that no understanding of price in a social marketing context existed no mention of it in the public-education campaign. No recognition that organized activities required effort by each government agency and community group that chose to organize. Price was not part of the campaign at this point.	Distribution included channels for getting the information kits, posters, and booklets to the targeted publics. Distribution concentrated on public sector, educational institutions and NGOs. The private sector was not emphasized.

1990-91	Slogans:
• Minister presented eight awards for Excellence in Race Relations	**1989**
• English and French general commercials featuring the slogan, "Racism Hurts"	*Together We're Better—Let's Eliminate Racial Discrimination in Canada*
• Department developed information kit for students to get involved with essays and poster contests, workshops, displays, and debates around the theme of combating racism	**1990**
	Same as 1989
• 90 municipalities proclaimed March 21 and held special events	**1991**
• 80 federal institutions organized activities in both headquarters and regions to commemorate the day	*Together We Can Stop Racism*
• 60 NGOs provided support to the March 21 Campaign by organizing activities to commemorate the day	**1992**
	Same as 1991
1991-92-93	**1993**
• Public awareness events were slightly modified from the previous years. Similar activities continued.	*Together We're Better—Let's Stop Racism*

TABLE 1 (*continued*)

Target Market	Strategic Plan	Relationships Partnerships	Explicit Exchange	Was Evaluation done?	Findings of Evaluations
No formal research conducted on a target market or group. No specific delineation of target markets. However focus tended to be youth, community organizations, and opinion leaders.	No strategic plan. 1992 external evaluation recommended a strategic planning process to: – identify issues of program ownership – assist with resource allocation – identify constraints – develop specific targeting	**General** • NGO's • Other government agencies • Educational Ministries **Specific** • Smith Corona (but no emphasis on private sector partnerships) – Canadian Advertising Foundation of Canada – Canadian Association of Broadcasters – Canadian Association of Police Chiefs – Canadian Ethno-cultural Council – Boys and Girls Club of Canada – Federation of Canadian Municipalities	There was no explicit exchange. The 1992 evaluation report notes that within a context of an awareness campaign, March 21 was successful. It was *not considered as a social marketing campaign.* The terminology of social marketing is beginning to appear in the programs' nomenclature. During 1993, vocabulary of social marketing became more prevalent. Also, during this time there were rapidly increased expectations and demands on the programs reach and grasp. – During this time, March 21 is referred to as a "campaign."	Internal evaluations were done annually. These consisted of fairly informal assessments of how many posters, information kits, etc. were distributed, how many media messages developed and used. The first external evaluation was done in 1992.	**Need for:** • Strategic Planning • Business planning (match resources to priorities and objective) • Need for use of marketing research–a formalized approach to program testing and assessment (e.g., use evidence to assess effectiveness of programs components • Need for more partnerships and sponsorships to help with resources needed to reach program goals. • Need for tailoring the program to the target group • Need for improved distribution, especially in logistical control, to move the materials out to targeted markets

TABLE 2. Transition to Social Marketing

Product	Promotion			Pricing	Distribution Channels
Products began to be developed to meet the needs of target markets	Tools	Messages	Media/Communication		
1994-96 Evidence in planning and strategy documents that beginning to recognize a more social marketing definition of product as stopping racist behaviors among Canadians. Still considerable carry-over from previous approach that products are booklets, posters, etc. **1996-97** Stop Racism video competition targeted to youth target market (with Panasonic). Product encouraged youth to demonstrate anti-racist behaviors in a tangible way–through video.	**1994-96** Booklets and posters for school-aged youth continued Public awareness events continued Web site introduced in 1996 **1996-97** Booklets and posters suggesting activities for school-aged youth continued T-shirts–Benetton provided risk capital and sold them	Messages becoming more consistent over time–re now more consistent between different media types Verbal and visual messages are more hard hitting. The messages were not actionable but becoming more so in 1997. **1996** The verbal message: *"Together to Change the World"* – accompanied by visual imagery–*the crocuses*	New ad agency was hired Initiatives from previous years continued (booklets, posters, information kits) **1997-2000** Stickers of "the Hand" supporting the March 21 brand were introduced and distributed Radio and television messages developed and broadcast reflecting more consistent messages and March 21 brand. Much/Music and Musique Plus aired commercials and 30- second edited versions of the winning entries from the video competition	Still no indication that the target markets pay a price in order to adopt the product was recognized in the program design and implementation	Distribution grew from public sector, educational institutions and NGOs to include the private sector–extending the reach of the program. Distribution channels became more intensive including 1-800 phone and Web site Private sector partners used to support the development and distribution of promotion items (i.e., Benetton re: t-shirts; Royal Bank re: posters; Roots, etc.)

TABLE 2 (*continued*)

Product	Promotion			Pricing	Distribution Channels
Products began to be developed to meet the needs of target markets	Tools	Messages	Media/Communication		
1997-98 Information kits targeted **to teachers** to use in curriculum suggesting activities for school-aged youth to make anti-racist behaviors tangible in the classroom. **1998-1999** Cyber petition was launched–asking youth as key target market to demonstrate anti-racist support by supporting petition. **1997-2000** Explicitly began asking for a behavior change *"Racism Stop It."* Supported by visual imagery in all communications materials. March 21 is being treated and described as a brand– supported by consistent promotional and visual images.	**1997-98** Posters **targeted to teachers** to use in curriculum suggesting activities for school-aged youth Introduction of events to increase awareness of anti-racism message to target groups (Raptors, Roots Against Racism, etc.) **1998-1999** Youth-focused campaign **targeted teachers** with activity suggestions to engage students in an ongoing dialogue of issues on racism (requests for these materials increased 32% over previous year) Development of Web Site — Web site is visited by users in 13 countries, received 786,900 hits	**1997-2000** The verbal message–becoming more a request for action from the target market– *Racism. Stop It!* The visual imagery– **Hand used in support of the Racism. Stop It! verbal message.**			**1997-2000** Internet became much more important way of distributing tools intended to encourage anti-racist behaviors Toll-free phone and fax lines for orders for promotion items, kits, and information

Target Market	Strategic Plan	Relationships Partnerships	Explicit Exchange	Was Evaluation Done?	Findings of Evaluations
Target groups were specifically defined as: • The media • Community organizations • Teachers • Youth 13-17 • The general public While the general public is not a specific target market, the transition to specifically targeting media, community organizations, and teachers and youth show movement toward more of a social marketing approach	No strategic plan. However, both the researchers' evaluations and an external evaluation of the program conducted in 1999 noted that implicit objectives were observable and could be identified throughout various internal documents. – March 21 is beginning to be referred to as a program/ brand rather than a campaign.	This period was marked by an increased emphasis on relationships and partnerships. A number of these are listed below. ***General*** • NGOs • Government agencies • Educational ministries • The private sector ***Specific*** • The Canadian Association of Broadcasters • Canadian Association of Police Chiefs • Canadian Teachers' Federation • CBC • Much Music • Musique Plus • The Royal Bank • Benetton • Roots Panasonic • Sympatico (not after 1998) • Tribute Teen • Famous Players • Vik Recording • Canadian Film Centre	There was little explicit exchange between the target and the government agency ***but there was an exchange*** between private organizations and the government agency. The private organization received advertising opportunities with the target in exchange for financial contributions to the program.	Internal evaluations were done annually. The second external evaluation began in 1997 and was published in 1999.	Analysis by the research team as well as the external evaluation published in 1999 noted the following: • Need to address logistics in getting the material out to target markets • Increased use of marketing research resulted in a shift in the promotion messages—members of ethnic groups felt the softer images were inappropriate and idealistic. This led to change in the product and the accompanying images which became much harder (Stop Racism and the Hand as compared to the previous softer images). • It is important that the message leads to action • Market research also showed need for stronger branding (e.g., the mention of March 21 Campaign confuses people. People don't know what the date stands for and they don't know if it is a one-time or annual event)

Social Marketing Ideas among the March 21 Staff). This was accomplished by rapidly expanding the role of private-sector sponsors/partners. Many of the elements designed and introduced during the early public-education phase continued on throughout the 1990s even as the language and tools of social marketing began to appear in the program materials, strategy, and evaluation documents.

3. *Social Marketing Techniques and Practices Evolved.* Over time social marketing principles (and the language of social marketing) were incorporated in the campaign, so that by 1999-2000, many of the most important features of a social marketing approach were integral to the program's activities. From its inception, the March 21 Campaign shared some characteristics of a social marketing campaign (such as the aspiration to change behavior as well as attitudes). After 1994-95, program staff made more extensive and more self-conscious use of social marketing techniques, including marketing research. The incentive for increased adoption of social marketing appeared to be twofold:

- Increased expectations regarding the reach of the program accompanied by a period of significant resource constraints. Under these conditions, senior managers became more aware of the concept and approaches of social marketing and viewed it as attractive in these circumstances.
- The first external evaluation of the program showed many elements of success within the context of a public-education program. This external evaluation made recommendations (see Table 1) to adopt social marketing approaches.

The social marketing features that were incorporated include increased emphasis on clear and specific target identification as well as increased development of marketing strategy around three of the four Ps.

The authors note that the external evaluation done in 1992 (early in the campaign) found fairly low awareness of the March 21 Campaign in both the youth and the adult markets, but that a majority of Canadians think that racism exists in Canadian society and that they personally can make a difference in eliminating racial discrimination. The 1999 evaluation showed that measures of level of branding and campaign awareness among the general public improved since 1992 when they were last measured (Canada,

Department of Canadian Heritage, 1999). However, it also showed that the March 21 brand still confused people–many don't yet know what it stands for. Higher levels of awareness of the campaign and its theme and products were found among the campaign's youth target market. For the most part, the 1999 evaluation measured different outcome variables than the earlier study, so it becomes challenging to make comparisons with measures in 1992 with a view to noting whether the use of social marketing tools and principles made a significant difference. The evaluation in 1999 notes strong support for the campaign among direct users of campaign products (educators and others). This evaluation also notes the need for more emphasis on showing direct benefits to targeted individuals of adopting alternative new behaviors. There is increasing acceptance and awareness that racism is "bad," that it should be stopped, and that individuals have a role stopping it. The later evaluation reflects a social marketing perspective that was absent in the early years by focusing on the branding measures, and the need for behavior changes, rather than just building awareness.

4. *Development of Strategy and Thinking around the 4 Ps.* More extensive distribution approaches were developed, as well as considerable development of all aspects of promotion. The promotion element became more sophisticated and messages more actionable on the part of targeted groups. Professional advertising-agency assistance was engaged to develop promotional messages.

A special comment regarding the development of the ideas of product strategy is warranted. First, in the early years (Phase 1), as shown in Table 1, the product was conceived as consisting of posters, brochures, and competitions that promoted the message of working together and building inclusive communities. In social marketing frameworks, these are more commonly regarded as promotional vehicles rather than as products. As social marketing ideas, tools, and thinking began to take hold, this early approach to defining the product began to change, albeit slowly and not completely. Gradually the notion that the product was intangible (anti-racist behavior on the part of Canadians) began to take hold. Further, recognition that one needs to try to understand the benefits consumers are really seeking (Andreasen and Kotler, 2003, 313) began to be observed. Documentation revealed stronger indication that products and promotional vehicles were designed with the needs of specific target markets in mind (i.e., it was recognized that if teachers were going to request and utilize kits designed to conduct school projects and videos involving discussion of the benefits of inclusion of all racial groups in schools and communities, then developing such products to meet the specific needs of teachers was required). As well, during the mid 1990s, March 21 began to be recognized and referred to as a brand. Multi-year consistency was considered as important in supporting this brand. Further, the symbol of the raised hand started to become a symbol associated with the March 21 brand. Terms such as "positioning" began to be observed within the strategy documents referring to product strategy. The weakest element in the social marketing strategy is a lack of understanding of the pricing component and the development of strategy concerning price.

The development of relationships/partnerships increased markedly and attempts at partnership development incorporated both organizations from the public sector as well as the private sector. Partnerships became a key cornerstone of the March 21 Campaign in the face of declining government resources. The notion of clearly identifying an explicit exchange with the target market is emerging, but the benefit to targeted groups for engaging in anti-racism behaviors is still not explicitly a part of the strategy. The use of marketing research has increased and evaluation has become more embedded in the campaign over time and changes to the campaign appear to be based on the results of previous evaluations.

5. *Some Social Marketing Practices Are Still Absent.* Some of the major social marketing features that are still absent include:

- explicit definition of the nature of the proposed exchange(s) with the target market,
- a clear understanding of pricing within the context of the campaign, and
- consistent tailoring of products and communication to specific target markets and further development of a strategic plan.

If one holds to the strict requirement that all program elements must be focused on eliciting behavior changes rather than settling for changes short of that goal (i.e., changes in attitudes), then it is important to recognize that this did not happen. However, considerable movement occurred during the evolution to social marketing period toward achieving this goal. The product was seen more as asking targeted consumers to stop racist behaviors. There was increased recognition of the costs of engaging in this behavior (i.e., the costs to teachers of acting as change agents) and attempts made to decrease the costs and increase the rewards. Promotion and product strategy more consistently attempted to achieve this behavior change.

Diffusion of Social Marketing Ideas Among the March 21 Staff

While the written documentation provided little information specifically noting *how* social marketing ideas were diffused among the staff, it becomes clear from the analysis of the features of the program that the staff and managers responsible for the program *were adopting* many key social marketing ideas. These findings then begged the questions of why were social marketing concepts, ideas, language, and tools adopted at that time, and how were they adopted.

How Social Marketing Was Diffused. First, the written documentation showed that one of the key agents of change was outside consulting groups engaged by the program management to provide evaluation of the program and recommendations for future strategy development. The first external evaluation in 1992 used much of the language of social marketing—encouraging both the development of a strategic plan and the use of business planning (matching resources, priorities, and objectives), as well as providing the first formalized program testing with accompanying recommendations that this continue. Further, this report used and encouraged the language of segmentation and target marketing.

Insights from the interviews were also important in understanding more about this diffusion process. These interviews suggested that several key managers within the unit managing the March 21 Campaign (the Multiculturalism Secretariat) acted as change agents in promoting the adoption of social marketing. These managers organized training for managers in the unit on the broader topic of marketing generally, and how it could be used in the Secretariat, as well as social marketing specifically and how it could be effectively utilized. At least one major (multi-day) training session was organized during the mid-1990s, which brought in external consultants to provide this training. Interviewer comments revealed that at least one manager in the unit in the mid-1990s had some professional training in marketing, but that the majority of the managers and staff within the unit were not highly knowledgeable about marketing or social marketing. However, management and staff were described as more than willing to use these tools to achieve goals within their unit. In order to understand these views, the interviews were designed to probe more deeply into understanding the work environment and context during the 1990s.

Why Social Marketing Was Adopted. The interviews revealed a great deal about underlying motivations for adopting a social marketing approach during the mid- to late-1990s within the Multiculturalism Secretariat. All interviewees noted that the years 1992-95 were "extremely tumultuous ones in the public service of Canada." The federal government at that time was undergoing a process known as "program review," which engaged all departments and agencies in a thorough reconsideration of their activities. In the same period until 1995, major efforts were made to reduce the size of the public-service workforce and considerable reductions in staff were made. Across the entire public service, departments were reformed and reconsolidated. Not surprisingly, during this period of downsizing, consolidation, and reorganization, written information and documentation is most scanty. However, the interviews and documentation analyses showed that in 1993, the Multiculturalism program was folded into the new Department of Canadian Heritage. The interviews also unanimously revealed that the March 21 Campaign was "rethought, refocused, and regenerated." The major shift at this time was a new emphasis on social marketing, featuring an increased reliance on market research, targeting, branding, and partnerships. It may be surprising that during this time of major turmoil, one would find an interest in and openness to social marketing. It was precisely this turmoil, however, that sowed the seeds for acceptance of social marketing as managers and staff, in the words on one interviewee, were highly motivated "to achieve their objectives in an atmosphere of declining resources." Interviewees suggested that the staff believed that they "should be breaking new ground in order to reach their objectives even though it might be risky to do so." The interviews as well as discussions occurring at meetings (where researchers acted as observers) also revealed that staff were working extremely hard during this period of uncertainty and that their openness to social marketing at this time was particularly strong as a result of the widespread public-sector need "to do more with less." Social marketing was seen as a way to accomplish a new start and expansion of the program, one that would embrace the public service thinking at the time of doing more with less.

In summary, a confluence of factors promoted the adoption of social marketing into this program at the time–major reorganization of government which promoted a rethinking of the March 21 Campaign, accompanied by an increased public-sector acceptance and consciousness of marketing and social marketing as a way of doing more with less. In this atmosphere of interest and willingness to utilize such approaches to achieve public-sector goals, management engaged outside consultants to provide much of the information and education about social marketing that enabled managers and staff to utilize it and incorporate it into the future of the March 21 Campaign.

SUMMARY, CONCLUSIONS, AND DISCUSSION

The research shows that the March 21 Campaign began as an internally funded Canadian federal government public education program that gradually took on many, but not all, of the characteristics of a social marketing program. Incentives for this adoption appeared to be the desire to increase the effectiveness of the program while coping with significant resource constraints as a result of the major federal government program-review exercise from 1992-95. As a result of this program review, the March 21 Campaign underwent a review and refocus that involved major changes that incorporated many elements of social marketing. To build internal management expertise concerning social marketing, outside consultants provided education and consulting advice that enabled the adoption of these social marketing ideas.

The program's evolution developed in two phases: Phase I: Getting Started: The Public Education Years, 1988-1993, and Phase II: The Shift From Public Education to Social Marketing, 1994-1999. The first phase revealed a program where the emphasis was on a public-education campaign concerning racism. The primary strategy centered on promotion, and considerable development of promotional strategy categorized this phase. From a social marketing perspective, there was no real segmentation or targeting of markets, market research, or conceptualization of exchange, pricing, and only minimally developed distribution strategy. The second phase showed a marked increase in characteristics that typify social marketing. These include increased segmentation and target marketing, product development aimed at specific targets, increased development of relationships/partnerships, increased development of distribution channels, market research, and an increased use of social marketing terminology in the documents describing the program.

It is clear that the program has not evolved to the point where it exhibits all the characteristics of social marketing. Most noticeably lacking are the notion of an explicit exchange, and the development of pricing strategies.

This case suggests that, at least within the Canadian federal public service, it may be possible for a social marketing program to evolve from a more traditional public-education campaign. In this case study, the department began an internally funded program to combat racism. The research shows that the program began as a fairly traditional public-education program (that evolved over time for several reasons outlined in the article) to encompass more of a social marketing approach. This social marketing evolutionary pattern may not be the norm, or represent the traditional pattern of development of social marketing programs. More commonly, social marketing programs are viewed as being developed by social agencies and/or governments who then apply for external funding which is needed to manage and implement the program. In developing future theory, it is important to recognize the possibility of the existence of alternate patterns for the development of social marketing programs. This case suggests that such evolutionary patterns may be possible in other situations that might most closely mirror the one under study.

Other situations that come to mind that might most closely parallel this research case would be those where governments are internally funding existing public-education programs that are attempting to promote attitude and/or behavior changes. Some examples in the Canadian context might include West Nile public-information programs developed and managed by a number of governments throughout the country. These programs most often include a variety of communication tools such as brochures, fact sheets, Web-site information, as well as television advertisements, for example. Social marketing approaches and tools might be useful to supplement or enrich current approaches for encouraging Canadians to protect themselves by selecting and wearing appropriate insect repellant as well as cleaning up around their houses in order to destroy mosquito-breeding habitats. Energy-conservation public-education/information programs are also frequently undertaken by governments at all levels to inform Canadians about effective energy conservation practices. Again, taking more of a social marketing approach in these programs might effectively encourage Canadians to change their behaviors regarding a wide variety of energy-conservation practices ranging from use of energy efficient light bulbs, adding insulation to residences, to turning off lights when leaving a room. At present it is not known how wide-ranging such possibilities are in other jurisdictions around the world, but this research suggests that it is worthwhile to investigate the prevalence of such possibilities.

If it can be shown that this pattern is not an isolated occurrence, and that social marketing programs may be built on the backs of other programs, then it may be worthwhile to market social marketing in such situations. In the face of barriers to the adoption of social marketing (Andreasen, 2002; Rogers, 1995), a potential strategy for "marketing" social marketing as a behavior change strategy is to recognize this evolutionary or morphing pattern and to assist in its progress. Such a strategy would involve attempting to introduce social marketing tools and ways of thinking into existing public-education programs. Barriers to adoption of social marketing are not completely eliminated through this evolutionary approach–lack of understanding and suspicion about what marketing might accomplish and how it might be utilized may still exist among upper management levels (Andreasen, 2002). However, slowly evolving a program into social marketing may effectively overcome many of the barriers that may prevent its adoption initially (Andreasen, 2002). Diffusion of innovation theory (Rogers, 1995) supports this view by showing that diffusion of innovations is more rapid and successful when adoption of an innovation is seen as compatible with previous values and ways of doing things (building upon public education may provide this base), and offers a relative advantage (change agents may slowly introduce aspects of social marketing that can be seen to offer advantages compared to the current approach).

This research points to an interesting "big-picture issue" related to the fact that a non-marketing approach eventually developed into a more customer-focused marketing program. The benefits of this approach from the government-implementation point of view appear to have included a greater comfort level with public education. At a time when customer-focused marketing approaches may have been perceived as much more risky, public-education campaigns were viewed as quite comfortable (many precedents having gone before) and seen as quite safe. The trade-offs may very well have been not moving ahead at all at the time if the choice had been a social marketing campaign or nothing. Since the inception of the March 21 public-education program in 1989, the social marketing approach has become much more accepted as a legitimate approach for influencing behaviors in the Canadian public service, yet it still suffers from many barriers (noted above) to its full-fledged adoption.

It is also important to note, however, that even after 12 years, a number of the important characteristics of a social marketing program were still absent from the March 21 Campaign. Several possible reasons for this lack of total adoption of social marketing must be considered. Lack of understanding of social marketing on the part of senior management may still exist and this may explain why several key aspects of social marketing are still missing. It is also possible that program managers do not believe that all elements of a social marketing program are appropriate in the context of a government-sponsored anti-racism program. Managers may believe that a full-scale marketing program may not be appropriate–perhaps it is still seen as being potentially too manipulative–so they purposefully back off from full-scale social marketing. Further research is needed to fully understand the reasons for this finding.

This research is limited to a single case, so it is important to recognize the need to do future research to show whether this pattern of the evolution of social marketing is common in other sectors, not-for-profit organizations, and countries. It is also important to determine the extent to which full-scale social marketing or partial social marketing programs are the result of such evolution and the reasons for this. Future research is also required to focus on how social marketing ideas become diffused among managers of programs that have not previously utilized them. Such research can provide baseline data to be used in future strategy development to increase the effective utilization of social marketing as a tool for affirmative change.

REFERENCES

Andreasen, Alan R. (2002), "Marketing Social Marketing in the Social Change Marketplace," *Journal of Public Policy & Marketing, 21*(1) 3-13.

Andreasen, A.R. and P. Kotler (2003), *Strategic Marketing for Nonprofit Organizations*, Upper Saddle River, NJ: Prentice Hall, Sixth Edition.

*Canada, Department of Canadian Heritage, *March 21 Surveys of Youth: Comparison of Pre-Launch and Post-Launch Impact Measures,* prepared by Fernando Mata, Strategic Research and Analysis, Multiculturalism/CCI, Draft: 18 May 2000.

*Canada, Department of Canadian Heritage, *Segmentation Analysis of Audiences of the March 21 Campaign,* prepared by Fernando Mata, Research and Business Planning, Multiculturalism/CCI, 18 May 2000.

*Canada, Department of Canadian Heritage, *Tenth Annual Report on the Operation of the Canadian Multiculturalism Act*, February 1999.

*Canada, Department of Canadian Heritage, *Segmentation Analysis of Audiences of the March 21 Campaign,* prepared by Fernando Mata, Research and Business Planning, Multiculturalism/CCI, 30 April 1998.

*Canada, Department of Multiculturalism and Citizenship, *An Evaluation of the March 21, 1992 Anti-Racism Campaign*, Final Report, prepared for Program Evaluation Directorate, prepared by Tao Research Associates Inc., September 1992.

*Canada, Department of Multiculturalism, *An Online Media Analysis: Multicultural-ism*, Earnscliffe Research and Communication, March 1996.

*Canada, Department of Canadian Heritage with assistance from Effie Panousos, Citizens' Participation Directorate, *Canadian Identity Sector: Attitudes Toward Diversity in Canada in the Context of Social Cohesion*, Margaret Adsett and Michael Willmott, Policy Coordination and Strategic Planning; Canadian Identity Sector, June 8, 1999.

*Canada, Department of Canadian Heritage, *March 21 Campaign, MuchMusic/MusiquePlus*, Partner Web Sites, Interim Report, prepared by Scott Thornley + Company, January 12, 1999.

*Canada, Department of Canadian Heritage, *March 21 Campaign, MuchMusic/MusiquePlus*, Tribute Partner Web Sites, Interim Report, prepared by Scott Thornley + Company, March 3, 1999.

*Canada, Department of Canadian Heritage, *March 21 Campaign, MuchMusic/MusiquePlus*, Web Sites, Final Report, prepared by Scott Thornley + Company, April 1999.

*Canada, Department of Canadian Heritage, *Establishing Performance Priorities for the Multiculturalism Program*, Tarik Ali Khan for The Multiculturalism Program, July 23, 1999.

*Canada, Department of Canadian Heritage, *Evaluation of March 21 Campaign for the International Day for the Elimination of Racial Discrimination*, Summary Report (Vol. 2), Corporate Review Branch, July 1999.

*Canada, Department of Canadian Heritage, *Evaluation of March 21 Campaign for the International Day for the Elimination of Racial Discrimination*, Best Practices for Social Marketing Campaigns (Vol. 1), Corporate Review Branch, July 1999.

*Canada, Department of Canadian Heritage, Multiculturism, *Racism. Stop It!* Information Booklet, March 21.

*Canada, Department of Canadian Heritage, *March 21–International Day for the Elimination of Racism: An International Comparative Review of Initiatives and Programs*, Heather De Santis, International Comparative Research Group (ICP), Strategic Research and Analysis (SRA), Strategic Planning and Policy Coordination, July 1996.

*Canada, Patrimoine canadien, Mathieu Da Costa Awards Program, Canadian Heritage, Canadian Teachers' Foundation, *Mettons fin au Racisme! Le 21 mars*, Guide a l'intention des enseignants, Niveau secondaire, Multiculturalisme, 1996.

*Canada, Patrimoine canadien. *Mettons fin au Racisme. Le 21 mars,* Guide a l'intention des enseignants, Niveau primaire, Multiculturalisme, 1996.

*Canada, Department of Canadian Heritage Multiculturalism, *Policies and Programs in Australia, United States, United Kingdom, Europe, and Malaysia* (with summaries in English and French), Karim H. Karim, PhD, International Comparative Research Group (ICP), Strategic Research and Analysis (SRA), Strategic Planning and Policy Coordination, October 1996.

*Canada, Department of Canadian Heritage, *Multiculturism, Immigration and Racism: Selected Public Opinion Poll Findings in Canada 1991-99*, (Summary contains syndicated as well as public results. Use discretion), compiled by Fernando Mata and Margaret Adsett, Multiculturalism/CCI, Draft: 29 July 1998.

*Canada, 2000 Thornley + Company and Northstar Research Partners, *National Stop Racism Video Competition*, prepared for Department of Canadian Heritage, July 1999.

*Canada, Groupaction Gosselin Strategic Communications, *Racism. STOP IT!* Action 2000, National Media Relations Plan, Final, August 1999.

*Canada, Department of Canadian Heritage, *Racism. Stop It!* Information Booklet, Action 2000.

*Canada, Department of Canadian Heritage, Multiculturalism, *Racism. Stop It! March 21*, Resource List, 1998.

*Canada, Department of Canadian Heritage, *Stop Racism Tour Canada Youth Challenge, Participants' Kit, French Version, Mettons fin au racisme! Tournee du Canada*, Le Defi-jeuness.

*Canada, Scott Thornley + Company Events Department, *Stop Racism! Tour Canada Youth Challenge, A Component of the Racism,* Stop It! Action 2000 Initiative, March 8, 1999, Revision 5.

*Canada, Department of Canadian Heritage Multiculturalism, *Stop Racism! National Video Competition 2000,* Media Partner Recommendation, Scott Thornley + Company + Events Department, July 27, 1999.

*Canada, The Evidence Series, *Facts about Multiculturalism*, Ethnic Identity Reinforces Attachment to Canada, May 21, 1998–Volume 1.

*Canada, *The International Day for the Elimination of Racial Discrimination*, Report on the 1998 March 21 Campaign, June 1, 1998.

*Canada, Department of Canadian Heritage, *Racism, Stop It! Teachers' Guide: Elementary Grades*, PCH 1996-159 E c.2

*Canada, Department of Canadian Heritage, *Racism, Stop It! Teachers' Guide: Secondary Grades*, PCH 1996-158 E c.2

*Canada, Department of Canadian Heritage, *Racism, Stop It! Teachers' Guide: Elementary Grades*, PCH 1997-2 E c.1

*Canada, Department of Canadian Heritage, *Racism, Stop It! Teachers' Guide: Secondary Grades*, PCH 1997-3 E c.2

*Canada, Department of Canadian Heritage, *Stop Racism. Tour Canada. Youth Challenge. Organizer's Kit*, PCH 1999-33 E c.2

*Canada, Department of Canadian Heritage, *Stop Racism. Tour Canada. Youth Challenge. Participant's Kit*, PCH 1999-34 E c.2

*Canada, Department of Canadian Heritage, *Racism. Stop It! Action 2000.* PCH 1999-35 E c.2

*Canada, Department of Canadian Heritage, *Racism. The International Day for the Elimination of Racial Discrimination, Stop It!* (Complete Information Kit) PCH 1999-6 E c.2

*Canada, Canada, Department of Canadian Heritage, *Mathieu Da Costa Awards Program*, Canadian Teachers' Foundation, 1999-2000 Mathieu Da Costa Awards Program, 2000

*Canada, Department of Canadian Heritage, News Release P-10/99-71, *"Montreal Youth Celebrate Diversity at Launch of Annual March 21 Campaign,"* October 6, 1999.

DeJong, W. (1989), "Condom Promotion: The Need for a Social Marketing Program in America's Inner Cities," *American Journal of Health Promotion, 3*(4), 5-16.

Hastings, G. (2003), "Relational Paradigms in Social Marketing," *Journal of Macromarketing, 23*(1), 6-15.

Kotler, P., and E. Roberto (1989), *Social Marketing*, New York: The Free Press.

Lwin, M.O., J.D. Williams, and L.L. Lan (2002), "Social Marketing Initiatives: National Kidney Foundation's Organ Donation Programs in Singapore," *Journal of Public Policy and Marketing, 21*(1), 66-77.

Madill, Judith (1999), "Marketing in Government," *Optimum The Journal of Public Sector Management, 28*(4), Spring, 9-18.

Maibach, E, and R.L. Parrott (eds.) (1995), *Designing Health Messages: Approaches from Communication Theory and Public Health Practice*, Thousand Oaks, CA: Sage Publications.

McKenna, J., K. Gutierrez, and K. McCall (2000), "Strategies for an Effective Youth Counter-Marketing Program: Recommendations from Commercial Marketing Experts," *Journal of Public Health Management and Practice, 6*, 7-13.

Ouchi, W. (1980), "Markets, Bureaucracies, and Clans," *Administrative Sciences Quarterly, 25* (March), 129-141.

Pechmann, C., and E. T. Reibling (2000), "Planning an Effective Anti-Smoking Mass Media Campaign Targeting Adolescents," *Journal of Public Health Management and Practice, 6*, 80-94.

Rogers, E.M. (1962), *Diffusion of Innovations*, New York: The Free Press of Glencoe.

Rogers, E.M. (1983), *Diffusion of Innovations*, New York: Free Press.

Rogers, E.M. (1995), *Diffusion of Innovations*, New York: Free Press.

Rothschild, M. (1999), "Carrots, Sticks, and Promises: A Conceptual Framework for the Management of Public Health and Social Issue Behaviors," *Journal of Marketing, 63*(4), 24-37.

Szulanski, G. (1996), "Unpacking Stickiness: An Empirical Investigation of the Barriers to Transfer of Best Practice Inside the Firm," *Academy of Management Review, 17*, 437-441.

Szulanski, G. (2000), "The Process of Knowledge Transfer: A Diachronic Analysis of Stickiness," *Organizational Behavior and Human Decision Processes, 82*, 9-27.

(* Indicates Department of Canadian Heritage Documents Used in The Research)

doi:10.1300/J054v17n01_02

North Carolina's Social Marketing Matrix Team: Using Social Marketing Concepts to Institutionalize Social Marketing Capacity in a State Health Department

Mike Newton-Ward

SUMMARY. The North Carolina Division of Public Health has employed traditional marketing concepts to increase the capacity of its programs to use the social marketing process. A Robert Wood Johnson Foundation Turning Point grant enabled this capacity building. During a three-year period there has been over a two-hundred-percent increase in programs attempting to use social marketing in the division. This article describes the division's application of social marketing concepts, reviews other theories useful to the incorporation of a social marketing approach in a social-change organization, makes suggestions for their application, and presents lessons learned. doi:10.1300/J054v17n01_03 *[Article copies available for a fee from The Haworth Document Delivery Service: 1-800-HAWORTH. E-mail address: <docdelivery@haworthpress.com> Website: <http://www. HaworthPress.com> © 2007 by The Haworth Press, Inc. All rights reserved.]*

Mike Newton-Ward is Social Marketing Consultant, North Carolina's Turning Point, North Carolina Division of Public Health, 1915 MSC, Raleigh, NC 27699-1915 (E-mail: mike.newton-ward@ncmail.net).

The author would like to thanks Jennifer Miller for her research assistance.

[Haworth co-indexing entry note]: "North Carolina's Social Marketing Matrix Team: Using Social Marketing Concepts to Institutionalize Social Marketing Capacity in a State Health Department." Newton-Ward, Mike. Co-published simultaneously in *Journal of Nonprofit & Public Sector Marketing* (Best Business Books, an imprint of The Haworth Press, Inc.) Vol. 17, No. 1/2, 2007, pp. 55-82; and: *Social Marketing: Advances in Research and Theory* (eds: Debra Z. Basil and Walter Wymer) Best Business Books, an imprint of The Haworth Press, Inc., 2007, pp. 55-82. Single or multiple copies of this article are available for a fee from The Haworth Document Delivery Service [1-800-HAWORTH, 9:00 a.m. - 5:00 p.m. (EST). E-mail address: docdelivery@haworthpress.com].

KEYWORDS. Social marketing, capacity building, public health, case study

BACKGROUND

Over the past four years, the North Carolina Division of Public Health (DPH) has developed the capacity of its programs to use social marketing to address various health issues. The division has utilized the social marketing process and core principles to "market social marketing." A Turning Point grant from the Robert Wood Johnson Foundation enabled this capacity building. The focus of the grant, based on results from a two-year planning grant process, was to increase the capacity of all programs within DPH to use "best practice" health communications and social marketing. The division received a smaller grant to join the Turning Point Social Marketing National Excellence Collaborative, with five other states. The mission of the collaborative is to provide national leadership to achieve integration of social marketing as a routine part of public health practice at all levels (Turning Point Social Marketing National Excellence Collaborative, 2000).

This funding allowed DPH to establish and fill a Full-Time Equivalent social marketing consultant position, and to have monies available to support planning and "intervention" activities that would develop a social marketing capacity. Under the auspices of the grant, the principle investigator established the Social Marketing Matrix Team in the spring of 2001. (This individual subsequently became the state health director. She remained the principle investigator for the duration of the grant, and has continued to support the development of social marketing capacity within the division). She charged the team to create a plan to institutionalize social marketing within all the programs of DPH and to develop the resources to implement the plan. Members of the team consist of staff representing various program areas, who currently are using social marketing, who are interested in learning to use it, or whom the division management considered to be good candidates for learning about social marketing and advocating for its use. It was envisioned that team members would both advocate for the use of social marketing in DPH, and develop their skill level in using social marketing, thereby enhancing the capacity of their program areas to do so. (The principle investigator chose to use the term "matrix" from the sense of the word representing a grid of interwoven resources from which something else can develop–in this case, increased social marketing expertise. As state health director she has created another "matrix team" to address school health issues.)

The social marketing consultant, hired through the Turning Point grant, is the convenor of the team. Other staff associated with the grant were a grant manager and an administrative assistant. The grant manager oversaw the daily operations of the grant, was involved in implementing the grant's objectives, and provided social marketing expertise. He is a member of the Matrix Team. This individual, who had a background in journalism and social marketing, was also manager of the North Carolina Public Health Awareness Program, and held a dual appointment with DPH and the School of Public Health at the University of North Carolina at Chapel Hill.

Since the division began its endeavors, Andreasen (2002) has discussed how social marketing processes can be used to address barriers to the adoption of social marketing and to advance its use. Although NC DPH chose to take this approach before the publication of this article, it provides a useful paradigm against which this article will later compare the experiences of the division. A review of Andreasen's approach is provided to establish the groundwork for that review.

Andreasen notes several barriers to the adoption of social marketing: "a lack of appreciation of social marketing at top management levels;" poor "brand positioning" (i.e., "social marketing as an approach to social change lacks clarity and is perceived by key influential people as having several undesirable traits"); "inadequate documentation and publicity of successes;" and a lack of "academic stature."

Additionally, Andreasen suggests that adoption of social marketing faces several forms of competition. It competes with the status-quo approach to doing things and with the view that an organized planning approach is not needed. Social marketing is seen by many as an individual level intervention to bring about social change. This puts it in competition with those who see social-change interventions needing to occur at the community level and structural level. The approach competes with other broad approaches to social-change interventions that can be used within each of those levels, such as education, law, and technology. Finally, as a "brand" of behavioral intervention for individual behavior change, social marketing competes with other conceptual approaches, including stages of changes, the health-belief model and strategic communications.

To address these barriers Andreasen proposes two solutions: branding social marketing to emphasize the unique benefits it offers to the endeavor of social change, and using marketing concepts to move organizational managers along the stages of change (Prochaska and DiClemente, 1983) to fuller acceptance and use of social marketing.

APPLICATION OF SOCIAL MARKETING CONCEPTS

The Social Marketing Matrix Team used core marketing concepts to promote the incorporation of social marketing into North Carolina DPH programs. This choice seemed inherently intuitive. Social marketing is about behavior change. NC DPH wanted to its staff to change their program-planning behaviors to include the social marketing approach. Therefore, why not use social marketing to "market" social marketing?

Basic social marketing concepts have been described in an increasing number of publications, trainings, and other resources (Andreasen, 1995; Donovan and Henley, 2003; Kotler, Roberto, and Lee, 2002; Turning Point Social Marketing Collaborative, U.S. Centers for Disease Control and Prevention, and Academy for Educational Development, 2004). The team applied traditional marketing concepts: target audience; behavioral objectives; audience research; barriers and benefits; competition; exchange; product, price, place, and promotion. As the team moved forward in its work, it kept in mind several definitions of social marketing. "Social marketing is the application of commercial marketing technologies to the analysis, planning, execution, and evaluation of programs designed to influence the voluntary behavior of target audiences in order to improve their personal welfare and that of their society" (Andreasen, 1995). "Social marketing is the use of marketing principles and techniques to influence a target audience to voluntarily accept, reject, modify, or abandon a behavior for the benefit of individuals, groups, or society as a whole" (Kotler et al., 2002). The team also heeded Smith's (1999) unusual perspective to, "Make the behavior Fun, Easy, and Popular for the target audience."

Planning Tools

The planning questions enumerated by Bryant (1997) guided the Matrix Team's development of preliminary goals and outcomes, initial selection of audiences, and formative research questions (see Figure 1). The team's initial decisions based on these questions are illustrated in Figure 2.

FIGURE 1. Social Marketing Planning Questions

GOAL: _____

1. To (achieve x), what do we want to **be changed or be different**?

2. What are the **outcomes**?

3. Who are the **audience(s)**?

4. What are the **barriers**?

5. What are the **facilitators**?

6. What do people **care about**?

7. What is the **effect of the environment**?

Used with permission. Bryant (1997)

Concepts

Target Audience. The team initially segmented DPH staff into program managers and program staff. Although staff would actually carry out social marketing interventions, the managers approved budgets and provided sanction for activities. Based on the formative research, the team further segmented the groups according to program area, their own familiarity with social marketing, and openness to using social marketing. The team chose to focus interventions on those who "definitely wanted to learn how to use social marketing now," and those who "might want learn about it at some point," as the easiest targets to move to action. Over the three-year period on which this article reports, individuals and programs have variously moved through the stages of change (Prochaska, Redding, and Evers, 2002) from precontemplation to contemplation, contemplation to action, and action to maintenance.

Audience research. Team members used formative research to find out how division staff viewed social marketing, what programmatic needs staff had that could be addressed by social marketing, and what barriers and facilitators existed to the adoption of social marketing. This was done in several ways. The team conducted a structured interview with both program staff and program administrators. Follow-up interviews were held with administrators, whom it was determined played a key role in adoption. Finally, the social marketing consultant used the team as an informal focus group of staff who were already interested in social marketing and who represented the various program areas. From

FIGURE 2. Initial Planning Decisions Made Using Social Marketing Planning Questions

GOAL: *Incorporate Social Marketing into the Work of the Division's Programs*

1. To incorporate social marketing into programs, **what do we want to be changed or be different**?

- Know what social marketing is
  - theoretical background
  - steps in process

- Change perception that marketing is costly
  - time
  - staff
  - money

- When social marketing is an appropriate intervention

- Make part of performance standards
  - Performance Management Work Plan (WPPR)

- State programs <u>encourage</u> local programs
  - State staff understand and practice it enough to promote social marketing

2. What are the **outcomes**?

- Encourage use internally
  - Social marketing is a **preferred** **tool** for grants, initiatives, interventions (educate granting agencies about marketing)

- Sanctioned from the top down
  - State health director, sections chiefs, branch heads

3. Who are the **audience(s)**?

- Program administrators

- Program staff

- Local health directors and program administration

- Training coordinators

- Consultants
  - Health education consultants (HEED)
  - Health promotion
  - School health
  - Social work
  - Nurses
  - Anyone in a training capacity

this process, the team identified benefits and barriers, product and placement issues, environmental influences, and ideas for promotion. The Matrix Team has conducted an additional round of formative research, since its initial inquiries, to further refine its marketing plan. The team used a "simplified elicitation methodology" (Middlestadt et al., 1996) that seeks to identify determinants of behavior by asking three pairs of questions: (1) what makes a behavior harder or easier to do; (2) what are the good things and bad things that happen when one does the behavior; and (3) who would approve or disapprove of the behavior? The research also asked which parts of the social marketing process and which concepts respondents regularly used, as well as what communication channels they preferred. The last series of research focused on administrators, using the questions posed in the simplified elicitation methodology. The research also inquired about their familiarity with the Social Marketing Matrix Team, whether they viewed social marketing as important to the current practice of public health and why, where they would seek help in using social marketing, their needs for social marketing training for themselves and their staffs, and media preferences.

Barriers. Identified barriers to using social marketing included: the perception that social marketing is not easy to integrate–that it is separate and apart from what staff are already doing; lack of knowledge; lack of time to attend trainings and other offering even if interest is there; lack of administrative support/understanding; directives from funders or institutional sources to use a certain approach (i.e., *not* social marketing).

Benefits. Identified benefits included: improved chance of sustained behavior change due to audience research and buy-in; improved accountability for use of scarce program resources because interventions are targeted; behavior change leads to improved health outcomes, which lead to accomplishment of program goals. This may lead to program recognition and continued or increased funding.

Related to benefits, the formative research also led to a better understanding of other facilitators of using social marketing (e.g., it is a policy or work-plan expectation, it complements what I already do, such as health education) and personal/professional motivations on which to build interventions: the approach is easy to do, fiscally responsible, and makes a difference for my target audience; staff buy into what their supervisor's value; and it provides professional development.

Competition. The major competition was using the status-quo approach to planning interventions, whatever that may be. There was a perception that social marketing is a passing fad. Two competing beliefs to using marketing were expressed: that the respondent, as a public-health professional, knew what was best for clients, and therefore did not need to conduct audience research; and variations of the belief that if people only are educated about what to do, they will do it.

The research yielded a rich array of data. A marketing plan was developed for each audience segment, with behavioral objectives and a mix of marketing strategies that addressed the issues identified for each audience in the formative research. Figures 3 and 4 illustrate interventions that the Matrix Team considered to lower the price of identified barriers and build on identified personal and professional motivations.

Behavioral objectives. Specific behavioral objectives were developed for each target group. For example, a behavioral goal for program staff was to "appropriately use a social marketing approach to plan,

FIGURE 3. Potential Interventions to Lower Price of Identified Barriers

What are the **barriers**?

- **Perception that social marketing is not easy to integrate, that it is separate and apart from what we are already doing**
  Rx: Education: what it is, see actual steps
  Rx: Concrete examples, technical assistance, hands-on support
  Rx: People: examples of staff integrating marketing into their work
  (e.g. use activity report developed by other staff as a way to document using social marketing as an intervention)

- **Lack of access to tools to perform social marketing**
  Rx: Worksheets, training, Web sites, newsletters
  Rx: Sample of model policy (local level) supporting use of social marketing
  Rx: Use people who are supportive and already using social marketing
  Rx: In training: identify key people who staff listen to/good trainers/ready adopters and get them on board

- **Lack of knowledge**
  Rx: Get on agendas at conferences
  Rx: Provide worksheets to guide staff through the marketing process

- **Lack of time to attend trainings, etc.**
  Rx: Integrate into things already attending
  Rx: Provide referrals to Listservs, Web sites as learning tools

- **This is just the latest fad**
  Rx: Endure
  Rx: Social marketing has been in use for 25 years
  Rx: Ask if what you are doing currently is successful
  Rx: Illustrate marketing's successes
  Rx: Focus on early adopters

FIGURE 4. Potential Interventions to Build Identified Personal and Professional Motivations

What do people **care about**?

- **It's easy for me**
  Rx: Case examples
  Rx: Worksheets, training, Web sites, newsletters that show how to use social marketing
  Rx: Sample of model policy supporting use of social marketing
  Rx: Use people who are supportive and already using social marketing
  Rx: In training: identify key people who staff listen to/good trainers/ready adopters and get them on board

- **This intervention works! It meets program goals. (It makes a difference.)**
  Rx: Case examples

- **It's fiscally responsible. Effective...good use of dollars**
  Rx: Case examples
  Rx: Provide Cost/Benefit Analyses of other social marketing interventions (e.g., Florida's Truth Campaign, WIC Breastfeeding, California 5-a-Day)

- **What their supervisors think (people buy into what their supervisors think/value)**
  Rx: Ask state health director to encourage program heads to incorporate social marketing
  Rx: Include social marketing activities in the work plans of program heads and staff
  Rx: Provide program heads and staff with examples of similar programs using social marketing
  Rx: Train program heads in use of social marketing
  Rx: Provide support/consultation to program heads as they incorporate marketing activities into their work

- **Professional development/learning**
  Rx: Provide social marketing-specific training opportunities (arrange for CEUs, certificates of completion, etc. where possible)
  Rx: Include social marketing training/content in other conferences/meetings (e.g., NC Public Health Association, Baby Love Conference, section staff meetings, etc.)
  Rx: Offer opportunities to audit UNC SPH courses on social marketing

(1) BACKGROUND
(1) APPLICATION OF SOCIAL MARKETING CONCEPTS
(2) Planning Tools
(2) Concepts
(3) *Target audience*
(3) *Audience research*
(3) *Barriers*
(3) *Benefits*
(3) *Competition*
(3) *Behavioral objectives*
(3) *Exchange*
(3) *Product*
(3) *Price*
(3) *Place*
(3) *Promotion*
(3) *Monitoring and evaluation*
(1) ADOPTING SOCIAL MARKETING IN SOCIAL CHANGE ORGANIZATIONS
(2) Top Managers as Target Audience
(2) Moving Audiences through Stages of Change
(2) Influencing Each Stage of Change

(2) Influencing Precontemplators
(2) Influencing Contemplators and Preparers
(2) Influencing Maintainers
(2) Increasing Benefits
(2) Lowering Costs
(2) Others Support the Use of Social Marketing
(2) Self-Efficacy
(2) Branding Social Marketing Against the Competition
(1) RESULTS OF NORTH CAROLINA'S EFFORTS
(1) IMPLICATIONS AND LESSONS LEARNED
(2) Using Marketing Concepts to Promote Social Marketing
(2) Building on Andreasen's Model for Marketing Social Marketing
(3) *Consideration of All Determinants of Organizational Change*
(3) *The Influence of the Environment*
(3) *Consider All Behavioral Determinants*
(2) Lessons Learned from North Carolina's Experience

implement, and evaluate behavior change interventions in their program area." Evaluation criteria were established for each objective. In this case, criteria included: Is the goal of the intervention behavior change? Is an attempt made to use audience research? Does the effort utilize the concepts of segmentation, exchange, and competition? Does the project consider all four Ps of the marketing mix? (And, even if the project uses only certain Ps, were all four considered?) Does the project have a monitoring and evaluation plan?

Exchange. As Donovan and Henley (2003, 25) note, "The concept of exchange has long been described as the core concept of marketing." All parties in the transaction perceive benefits and costs, which may be tangible or intangible. For a party to adopt a new behavior, the benefits must outweigh the costs (Bryant, 1997). As the Matrix Team has developed its mix of interventions, it has sought ways to ensure that something of value to the particular target audience is offered that outweighs the perceived costs, and that our interventions support the promise that a benefit will be received.

For example, program staff who "definitely wanted to learn how to use social marketing now" were the easiest group to move to change their behavior. They already perceived strong benefits to using social marketing: an opportunity for lasting behavior change in their target audience leading to improved health outcomes, which then would meet goals of their program and provide a sense of satisfaction; and improved accountability in use of funds and staff time. The barriers they experienced included a lack of knowledge about using the social marketing approach correctly; concern that it involved new steps or activities that would have to be superimposed onto already busy schedules; and a lack time to attend training, even though it was desired. To *emphasize the benefits,* the team positioned social marketing as a way to achieve the desired benefits in all communications that promoted either social marketing generally or training offerings specifically. The team reiterated these benefits in the training offerings, and used case studies and personal testimonies that illustrated these benefits. *To lower the costs,* the following interventions were offered to these specific concerns:

Lack of knowledge   "Social Marketing 101" training, consultation, and technical assistance to address specific application questions, access to social marketing publications, referral to the

	Georgetown University Social Marketing Listserv;
Concern about additional steps	Training and consultation that demonstrated which social marketing phases, concepts, and activities were similar to things staff currently were doing; case examples and personal testimonies from staff who had successfully integrated the social marketing process into their work; specific personal support and encouragement from the social marketing consultant; acknowledging the concern and reiterating the benefits the staff had cited as important;
Lack of time for training	Scheduling training over lunch; sanction from the state health director or the direct supervisor for taking time from other duties to attend training; using blast e-mails and social marketing bulletin boards as channels identified by staff for receiving information.

The costs to the Matrix Team and the social marketing consultant to offer these interventions were primarily financial, and the time to develop and conduct the offerings. (It should be appreciated that all team members except the social marketing members have full-time jobs in their programs with a variety of duties. Their work on the Matrix Team is additional, although it is a part of the work plans for some members.) The offsetting benefits for members included personal and professional satisfaction of promoting an approach that they strongly believed improves public health programs and ultimately the welfare of their target audiences; responding to an appointment to the team by the state health director; and an opportunity to use their unique skill set (e.g., planning skills, conducting training, developing creative materials). They saw the public health system benefiting by having a tool with which to develop interventions that support lasting behavior change, drive improvements in health indicators, and create an improved quality of life for people in the state.

Product. Kotler et al. (2002, 195) define product as "...the desired behavior and the associated benefits of that behavior. It also includes any *tangible products* and *services* developed to support and facilitate the target audience's behavior change." Our product is the appropriate use of the social marketing approach by staff to plan, implement, and evaluate behavior change interventions in their program area. This was positioned with the benefits identified as important by them, which could realistically be delivered by the use of social marketing, based on experience from the field: improved chance of sustained behavior change due to audience research and buy-in; improved accountability for use of scarce program resources because interventions are targeted; and behavior change leads to improved health outcomes, which lead to accomplishment of program goals. Tangible products and services developed to support the desired behavior included: on-site trainings; sponsoring staff to attend the annual Social Marketing in Public Health Conference at the University of South Florida; a mechanism for obtaining consultation from the Matrix Team; actual consultation; and the establishment of a social marketing library with relevant books and journals. An exciting recent development is the offering of training in the use of CDCynergy-Social Marketing Edition (Turning Point Social Marketing National Excellence Collaborative et al., 2003). CDCynergy-Soc. is an interactive, computer-based planning tool for developing, implementing, and evaluating social marketing interventions.

Price. Identified costs to using social marketing, and tactics to address them, are discussed in the section on exchange. Additionally, the financial cost of obtaining training and background publications were borne by funding from the Turning Point grant. Introduction of CDCynergy-Soc. into the division may help address price concerns about lack of knowledge, ease of use, and integration into current work.

Place. A place tactic that the Matrix Team has used is "be[ing] there at the point of decision-making" (Kotler et al., 2002). Program staff have many opportunities to choose to use a social marketing approach or some other planning approach. These often involve applications for new funding or the renewal of an existing grant. Team members keep track of these opportunities and have approached program personnel in advance of the event to explore whether a social marketing approach would be beneficial. Each month of the year is dedicated to numerous health programs or issues. The team has used blast e-mail, dedicated social marketing bulletin boards in division buildings, and personal contacts to share examples of social marketing applications to the health issues in that month, and to remind staff that the Matrix Team is available for consultation.

Several distribution strategies have been used, involving individual staff. Team members act as the liaison to their program areas about social marketing issues and information. The social marketing consultant has entrée into the division's programs to discuss marketing and deliver products. Trusted key individuals may be used to reach out to a certain program. Trainings variously have been offered as separate events or as a part of scheduled meetings or conferences.

Promotion. The team has used several promotion tactics to support the use of social marketing. Based on audience media preferences, the team uses blast e-mails to convey information and announcements. Dedicated social marketing bulletin boards have been set up at key locations in the buildings housing DPH. These are used to provide social marketing case examples, tips on use, and reminders of the Matrix Team's availability for consultation. The social marketing consultant and the grant manager give presentations to program management teams, and at the division's Public Health Management Team, on social marketing activities, benefits, and resources. They and the team members often engage key program staff and managers in one-on-one discussions. Word-of-mouth referrals from satisfied staff and programs to others have played a large role in encouraging the incorporation of social marketing into the division's programs.

The state health director has declared November "Social Marketing in Public Health Month" for the past two years. This has involved various promotional and educational activities, and provided the opportunity for additional audience research.

The team has bought social marketing textbooks and journals and distributed them to key staff. Because North Carolina participates in the Robert Wood Johnson Foundation Turning Point Social Marketing National Excellence Collaborative, the team has used the collaborative's products as they become available. These include: a "Social Marketing 101" PowerPoint training with case studies and participant exercises; a collection of case studies illustrating social marketing applications to public health, environmental, and other issues; a basic overview of the phases and concepts of social marketing; and a guide for program managers, with strategies for supporting the use of social marketing. These products have been useful in addressing the barriers identified by staff.

A promotional campaign with specific messages to promote social marketing has not been undertaken. Rather, the team has sought to frame its various activities in ways that address the benefits and barriers the audiences have identified, and to use specific terminology or phrasing if that has been identified (e.g., "accountability to funders" or "legislators," "social marketing gives you 'measurable results' " or "drives the needle," "you are already doing it"). The audience research led the team to focus on tactics to lower barriers and maximize benefits, and to use promotion to create a normative environment for social marketing.

These examples have focused primarily on the audience of program staff, and have reviewed selected tactics for the sake of brevity. The Matrix Team has conducted other interventions with staff, and separate, targeted interventions with program managers.

Monitoring and evaluation. In addition to using the core marketing concepts already discussed, the team monitors and evaluates the implementation of the marketing plan and its outcomes. Evaluation criteria are identified for each behavioral objective in the plan. The social marketing consultant follows up with recipients of consultation to gauge the extent to which they have used recommendations, and to identify additional areas for assistance. As the audience's needs or behavioral determinants have changed, the team has updated its intervention activities to be compatible. Additionally, the team has conducted a yearly SWOT (Strengths, Weaknesses, Opportunities, and Threats) analysis of its work in order to carry out strategic planning for the coming year.

ADOPTING SOCIAL MARKETING IN SOCIAL CHANGE ORGANIZATIONS

Andreasen (2002) offers a plan to promote the adoption of social marketing in social change organizations, which provides a paradigm against which to compare the experiences of NC DPH. To successfully market social marketing in social-change organizations, he proposes focusing on decision makers to move them through Prochaska and DiClemente's (1983) stages of change. Interventions need to address benefits, costs, others, and self-efficacy, what he has termed the "BCOS factors." Following Maibach and Cotton (1995), Andreasen suggests strategies with which to approach decision makers at each stage of change. He also advises branding social marketing to emphasize the unique benefits it offers to the endeavor of social change. NC DPH's experiences bear out many of Andreasen's proposed steps. Other conceptual approaches to incorporating social marketing into social-change organizations offer additional perspectives that can augment his paradigm. This article will compare NC DPH's experiences with each concept in Andreasen's (2002) framework, and will examine where other theories support or differ from his approach, where appropriate.

Top Managers as Target Audience

Andreasen chose top-level managers as the audience most in need of interventions in order to advance social marketing. Extensive formative research demonstrated that this group is often unaware of social marketing or does not appreciate the benefits it brings to the development of social-change initiatives. Conversely, the research indicated that staff implementing programs have shown greater acceptance of social marketing.

NC DPH found that both program managers *and* staff ("program doers") needed to be addressed in order to promote social marketing within the organization. There was some level of awareness among both groups that there was an approach called social marketing. However, there was great variety in the appreciation of the benefits of the approach and in an understanding of how to utilize it within the two groups. Managers provide administrative sanction to use specific planning approaches, and the fiscal resources to do so. Staff need the knowledge and skills to utilize social marketing processes. Because these determinants of behavior resided in both groups, NC DPH focused on both managers and staff as broad target audiences.

Diffusion Theory (Oldenburg and Parcel, 2002) adds support for selecting top managers as the primary audience. Managers are well situated to set the agenda for an organization, which is the first stage of the diffusion of innovations within organization. Additionally, to the extent that formal leaders exercise "opinion leadership" they can speed the adoption of an innovation. This is especially important when the innovation is perceived to negatively affect the allocation of resources, or when organization members are unsure of the outcome of adopting the innovation (Dearing, 2004). (For example, is social marketing perceived to strain existing personnel or fiscal resources, or remove resources that support, say, community outreach activities? Will the investment of effort truly lead to improved health outcomes?) However, to the extent that lower-level managers or program staff exercise opinion leadership, they would be audiences worthy of attention, also.

Kutz (2000) cited leadership as one of the major factors that influenced the Centers for Disease Control and Prevention (CDC) to build its social marketing capacity. She describes how various directors had the vision to realize that social marketing (and communications) were the tools needed to address emerging public-health problems; brought in outside expert resources to inform the Centers' marketing strategy formation; established a task force to explore the role of social marketing and health communication in the organization–and eventually an Office of Communication as a go-to resource; and finally, undertake a branding campaign for the organization and its work. Clearly, a focus on obtaining management buy-in to social marketing is important.

Moving Audiences Through Stages of Change

Andreasen classifies the adoption of a social marketing approach as a high-involvement behavior, that is, a behavior about which the audience cares deeply. It is often emotionally laden, and the audience will seek out a great deal of information and give much thought to the decision to change (Andreasen, 1995). He views these behaviors as coming about through stages, and proposes that interventions need to be crafted to match the stage the audience is in.

NC DPH found the Stages of Change model (Prochaska and DiClemente, 1983) useful for understanding our audiences' readiness to learn and use the social marketing approach, and to segment them for interventions. It provided a useful reminder to members of the Social Marketing Matrix Team that change *takes place over time* (Prochaska et al., 2002)–even if the audience is public-health practitioners! Diffusion Theory (Oldenburg and Parcel, 2002) offers a complementary paradigm of adopter categories (innovators, early adopters, early majority adopters, late majority adopters, laggards) with which to segment audiences for interventions. The theory supports the approach of segmenting by audience characteristics.

Influencing Each Stage of Change

Andreasen offers intervention ideas to address what he views as the dominate determinant of change for each change stage: correcting myths and preconceptions about social marketing that are barriers to adoption for precontemplators; addressing the BCOS factors for contemplators; supporting preparers/actors through existing networks of social marketers and "off-the-shelf " tools; offering reassurance to support the actions of maintainers through forums for sharing the results of social marketing interventions. DPH's Social Marketing Matrix Team found managers and staff at each stage, and used this information to segment the audience. The team chose to focus on contemplators and preparers as the easiest targets to move to action. (Staff who could be considered actors and maintainers were few, and tended to be those who made up membership of the Matrix Team.) This article will now examine interventions for each stage.

Influencing Precontemplators

Andreasen sees a major task with this segment as addressing myths and preconceptions that form barriers to the adoption of social marketing. He cites among these: "marketing is manipulative;" "marketers are shallow and unethical, and associating with them will diminish the stature of programs;" "marketing is too expensive;" "marketing is just putting different labels on what other brands have always done." The last two beliefs were evident in NC DPH's segment of precontemplators. Other prominent themes included: marketing is a new, unproven approach–a fad that will disappear; marketing is concerned only with those easiest to reach, while public health should be concerned with everyone, especially those most difficult to reach; marketing is long on process and short on action; and variations on "marketing is too expensive" (e.g., too time-consuming, too labor-intensive, too research-oriented.)

It is important to note that DPH also found some of these beliefs in our contemplator, preparer and actor segments as well, and they had to be addressed. These audiences, however, perceived significant benefits in social marketing, which served to counterbalance the perceived negatives. Thus, the negatives moved more into the category of costs that need to be lowered than barriers that precluded consideration of social marketing.

Influencing Contemplators and Preparers

Andreasen recommends focusing on the BCOS factors with contemplators, in order to position social marketing as being a significantly different tool for planning and implementing behavior change. NC DPH found that it was important to focus on BCOS factors with both contemplators *and* preparers. These stage constructs represent a temporal dimension–an intention to take action within the next six months or the next thirty days for contemplators and preparers, respectively (Prochaska et al., 2002). DPH's audience research showed that even those who were close temporally to taking action needed additional, specific information about benefits, costs, and sources of support in order to defend and cement their decision to incorporate a social marketing approach into their work. They also very much needed additional education and opportunities for practice in order to gain the knowledge, skills, and confidence to conduct "best practice" social marketing (the "self-efficacy" in the BCOS model).

Preparers (and actors) can benefit from the aid and influence of established social marketers, according to Andreasen. These resources and "off-the-shelf tools" can encourage these audiences that social marketing can be done easily and successfully. DPH heavily used the grant's manager, the social marketing consultant, and external practitioners, as well as publications, Web sites, PowerPoint presentations and the CDCynergy-Soc. software (Turning Point Social Marketing Collaborative et al., 2003), when it became available, to support staff at the preparation and action stages.

Diffusion Theory (Oldenburg and Parcel, 2002) identifies a set of attributes of an innovation that affect how quickly and to what extent the diffusion occurs. These parallel the benefits, costs, others, and self-efficacy–the BCOS factors. They lend support to the choice to focus on the BCOS factors, and offer another lens through which to plan successful interventions.

The BCOS factors are a distilled version of certain determinants of behavior: "benefits" and "costs" represent perceived and actual consequences of behavior; "others" refers to group, organizational, and cultural norms (this could reflect the organizational culture, or that of the professional discipline, as well as societal or ethnic affiliations); "self-efficacy" encompasses the skills and knowledge needed to use social marketing, as well as the sense that one can indeed successfully do what is required in social marketing. These determinants correspond to a subset of a list of behavioral determinants, codified by the Academy for Educational Development (AED) (Strand and Lewis, 2003), and based on work by Fishbein et al. (2001), that explain whether an individual will do a particular behavior. The complete list includes external determinants (policies, access, skills, actual consequences, cultural beliefs and values), and internal determinants (knowledge and beliefs, attitudes, perceived risk, perceived consequences, self-efficacy). The original list emerged from a consensus meeting sponsored by the National Institutes on Mental Health, which brought together "leading proponents of five major behavioral theories [social cognitive theory; health belief model; reasoned action; self-regulation, self-control; Subjective Culture and Interpersonal Relations] in order to identify a finite set of variables to be considered in any behavioral analysis" (Fishbein et al., 2001). The genesis of the meeting was to inform work on the AIDS epidemic.

Use of the BCOS model should lead to the development of helpful interventions because the model represents selected determinants of behavior. This author suggests, however, that one look at the full set of determinants as enumerated by AED. They are extremely helpful in suggesting areas for formative research to understand the determinants of a particular behavior, as well as suggesting potential points for interventions.

Influencing Maintainers

Maintainers "need reinforcement about the wisdom of their actions," according to Andreasen. He suggests that forums for sharing the results of social marketing interventions can be helpful. DPH found this to be true for the small number of staff who were in maintenance or those who moved into this stage, and utilized the social marketing Listserv, Matrix Team meetings, attendance at conferences, as well as e-mail and face-to-face communications.

Increasing Benefits

Andreasen suggests promotion of the benefits that comprise the unique strengths of social marketing as a strategy to influence contemplators: an audience orientation; a focus on behavior change as the bottom line; interventions tailored to audience segments, allowing efficient use of resources and more effective tactics; a range of intervention strategies in addition to promotion to lower the costs of behaviors and make them "fun, easy, and popular" (Smith, 1999). NC DPH also promoted these benefits as a necessary condition to enhance its audiences' understanding of social marketing, and to position social marketing as different from other tools for social change. While these generic social marketing benefits had prima facie appeal to some members of our audience, the DPH Social Marketing Matrix Team also found it necessary to translate them, or connect them, to terms that were meaningful to the target audiences (e.g., the improved chance of behavior change leads to improved health outcomes, which lead to accomplishment of program goals; positive improvement of health indicators leads to continued funding or program recognition; use of social marketing meets with approval of their supervisor)

Lowering Costs

"Finding talented help" is the primary cost associated with social marketing that Andreasen identifies. He notes that finding this help is becoming easier through venues such as the social marketing Listserv and other online sources, and through the increased willingness of private-sector marketers to work on social problems. However, in the case of NC DPH, the division wanted to nurture the "talented help" from within. These audiences associated a broader set of costs, specific to themselves, with incorporating social marketing into their work (e.g., a lack of knowledge about using the social marketing approach correctly; concern that it involved new steps or activities that would have to be superimposed onto already busy schedules; a lack of time to attend training; lack of supervisor support). Andreasen is correct that cost concerns have to be addressed. However, the unique costs relevant to each audience need to be identified through formative research–they may be different from the ones he identifies. Andreasen finds costs to be an important determinant of acceptance of social marketing at the contemplator level. North Carolina's experience suggests that costs need to be addressed for preparers and actors, too.

Others Support the Use of Social Marketing

NC DPH experience supports Andreasen's contention that the use of other persons and venues to support the adoption of social marketing is important. The division used internal resources, such as the Turning Point grant manager, the social marketing consultant and the Social Marketing Matrix Team. Important outside resources included the Turning Point Social Marketing National Excellence Collaborative, the Centers for Disease Control and Prevention and other federal programs that use social marketing, and other social marketing practitioners available through the social marketing Listserv and conferences such as the University of South Florida's annual Social Marketing in Public Health Conference. In North Carolina's case, the support of the state health director was a significant source of support from an administrative, non-social-marketing source. This serves as a reminder that the supportive "others" may be administrative champions–a source not to be overlooked!

Maibach (2000) discusses factors that support a social marketing perspective in social-change organizations. He includes among these: gathering the right mix of people needed to conduct the various activities that the social marketing process requires, such as audience research; using models of behavior change; and project management. It may be equally as important to gather the right mix of Andreasen's "others" to provide the various resources that are needed to support the development of new social marketers. These may include not only experienced social marketers, but those with good interpersonal skills who can provide quality consultation and coaching, individuals skilled at linking people and resources, and persons from the same professional discipline, health-topic area or personnel position who can be perceived as "like me."

Self-Efficacy

DPH found that building the knowledge, skills, and practice opportunities that lead to a sense of self-efficacy among managers and staff is central to the adoption of the social marketing approach. While attention to benefits, costs, and others may be construed to provide a mind-set receptive to social marketing, self-efficacy provides the engine to conduct the social marketing process.

Branding Social Marketing Against the Competition

Andreasen argues that a major strategy for promoting social marketing's acceptance in social-change organizations is branding it as having superior benefits to competing approaches for social change. He also suggests that social marketers identify ways in which their approach can complement and collaborate with other approaches. North Carolina's Social Marketing Matrix Team found using both methods helpful to promoting the incorporation of the social marketing into he work of DPH. It was necessary to "differentiat[e] social marketing as clearly and dramatically as possible" (Andreasen, 2002) in order to: establish that the approach was indeed different from, say, health communication; demonstrate that it offered a unique set of benefits that could help managers and staff accomplish things that were important to them (and which may have eluded them using other approaches); and, clarify that doing certain free-standing activities (e.g., conducting focus groups) did not constitute social marketing. Conversely, it was important to identify how the audiences already were doing some portions of the social marketing processes in their current approaches, in order to address the barrier that social marketing involved new activities that would have to be superimposed onto already busy schedules.

RESULTS OF NORTH CAROLINA'S EFFORTS

There is encouraging progress toward the team's goal of incorporating social marketing into the work of the division's programs. Over 50% of staff attending trainings requested additional consultation. During the first year of the Matrix Team's existence, seven programs sought consultation about 11 projects. Over the next two years, 17 programs requested consultation on 29 projects and grants, with requests for assistance occurring earlier in the planning process. The team believes this indicates an increased understanding that social marketing is a strategic process that requires time and resources to conduct as a "best practice," not something that is done the day before a grant application is due. For certain programs, it is becoming normative to request assistance in preparing a grant proposal on a recurring basis, or to request consultation on how to apply social marketing when a new health issue arises. Perhaps the most telling indicator of the team's success came recently in DPH's response to an RFA related to childhood overweight. The various programs that deal with issues affecting this health problem convened and decided that they wanted to submit a single application, and that the application should use a social marketing approach. They requested that the social marketing consultant and the Matrix Team take the lead in writing the application and in implementing it. The application subsequently was approved, and funded for three years.

IMPLICATIONS AND LESSONS LEARNED

Using Marketing Concepts to Promote Social Marketing

The experience of the North Carolina Division of Public Health's Social Marketing Matrix Team demonstrates how social marketing theory and concepts can be applied to promote the field of social marketing. The program provides a successful model for encouraging the growth and use of social marketing within a state health-department system or similar social-change organization. Social marketing *can* be used to market social marketing. Additionally, concepts from other theories, such as Stages of Stage and Diffusion Theory, can be helpful in developing strategies to promote the use of social marketing.

Building on Andreasen's Model for Marketing Social Marketing

Andreasen's (2002) framework offers useful guidance for using social marketing strategies to promote social marketing. His suggestion to brand social marketing offers a way to position it for continued development, and acceptance in social-change organizations. And he provides strategies for addressing the lack of appreciation of social marketing by organizational managers–an audience identified through formative research. Indeed, a number of his suggestions are borne out in NC DPH's efforts to incorporate social marketing into its programs. However, reviewing Andreasen's model in light of North Carolina's experience and other theoretical approaches suggests additional areas for an organization to consider that seeks to market social marketing.

Consideration of All Determinants of Organizational Change. Basil (2000) notes, in an introduction to a series of articles addressing the institution of social marketing in social change organizations, that a number of "structural 'upstream' and individual 'downstream' " forces effect change in an organization. He cites as upstream factors: learning within organizations that supports acceptance of new ideas; encouragement to adapt an innovation; changes in a state important to the organization, such as profits (for public health, this could be health indicators), that provide a reason to try something new; and new management, which brings an openness to trying new approaches. He reviews downstream factors such as: arrival of new employees who bring in new ideas; creation of ad hoc groups that generate new approaches from the "bottom-up;"staff education that provides exposure to different ideas. Because organizations are complex, layered entities they can be approached on many levels to create change (Steckler, Goodman, and Kegler, 2002). Indeed, interventions at multiple levels may be required to foment change. Those desiring to create a social marketing environment in an organization can undertake formative research to determine at which levels to intervene.

Diffusion theory also notes that successful diffusion of an innovation may require a multilevel change process that pays attention to the organizational level (Oldenburg and Parcel, 2002). These authors note that interventions in an organization can range from initiation of special programs to policy changes to changes in roles of personnel. Kutz (2000) relates how the CDC utilized staff teaching, workgroups, and creation of a new office in order to incorporate social marketing and health communication into CDC. Andreasen's steps focus on two of the upstream factors mentioned above by Basil: learning within organizations that support acceptance of new ideas; and encouragement to adapt an innovation. Because social change organizations are complex entities that may require multi-tiered interventions to effect change, the social marketer should give consideration to a wide variety of strategies that are supported by formative research.

The Influence of the Environment. Andreasen's framework acknowledges the influence of the environment in its attention to the role that "others" play in supporting the developing social marketer as an intervention. His choice of top-level managers recognizes their place as part of the environment affecting growth of social marketing in the organization. External and internal environmental influences are an important determinant of behavior; they deserve adequate consideration. In a review of factors influencing CDC's acceptance of social marketing (Kutz, 2000), four of the five factors cited were environmental changes. The stages of the diffusion of innovations in organizations (Oldenburg and Parcel, 2002) describe how the internal environment of an organization *interacts* with the innovation, both in selecting the innovation and in molding it to fit the organization's structure and objectives.

Social marketing is no stranger to considering the role of environmental influences on behavior. Kotler et al. (2002) state: "Mapping the social marketing environment early in the planning process makes it possible for social marketers to anticipate these forces and to develop strategies that minimize their impact and enable timely and orderly adaptations in the life cycle of the social marketing program." A SWOT analysis provides a useful tool for assessing both the internal and external environments in relation to a particular behavior.

Consider All Behavioral Determinants. There are many possible determinants of a set of behaviors. Social marketers and others wishing to effect behavior change should consider a range of determinants. This author has found the set of determinants described by Fishbein et al. (2001), discussed in the section Influencing Contemplators and Preparers, to be especially helpful for suggesting areas for formative research and possible intervention strategies. It has the benefit of being informed by several behavioral theories, which increases its applicability to different situations. Social marketers can also use this set of determinants to illustrate to managers and staff that communications-only interventions may not be sufficient to bring a desired behavior change.

Lessons Learned from North Carolina's Experience

This author previously has summarized lessons learned from NC DPH's experience (Newton-Ward, 2004), which other social change organizations can use to incorporate a social marketing approach into their work. These include:

- Link with others–Identify other staff who are interested in social marketing or open to learning about it. Joining with "fellow deviants" produces encouragement for one's efforts and can demonstrate to managers and other staff that this is not a "flash-in-the-pan" phenomenon.
- Look for natural opportunities–Use naturally occurring opportunities such as staff meetings or the announcement of a grant Request For Proposal to talk about social marketing and its benefits. Use case studies pertaining to program areas and health issues germane to those you work with to illustrate how social marketing can be utilized.
- Find out what people want–Find out what is important to managers and fellow program staff, and demonstrate how social marketing can meet their needs. For example, if fiscal accountability is important, show how formative research and audience segmentation can allow funds to be directed to the populations that are most ready to change. If staff want adoption of a new planning process to be easy, you might provide practical trainings, case studies with relevant applications or a "buddy system," pairing a staff member with a more experienced social marketer.
- Find a champion–It can be helpful to find someone at the management level who is supportive of social marketing. This person does not have to be the state health director, as is the case in North Carolina. However, it should be someone who can influence budget and other resource allocations, and who can provide administrative sanction for your activities.
- Create "buzz"–Do things that will create excitement around social marketing and that will generate interest and discussion. Use different media and places to promote social marketing. Continue to repeat messages. Identify ways to communicate about social marketing that are memorable and meaningful to your audiences.
- Remember to use good group process–The group you convene to promote social marketing is subject to the same group and organizational dynamics as any other group. These dynamics and norms occur and affect group functioning positively and negatively, whether you

attend to them or not. You should, therefore, manage them strategically and purposively to create a highly functioning, effective group. There are many reference books and classes that can help you do this.

- Continue to educate yourself–It is easy to get caught up in the daily demands of your job and neglect nurturing your own growth and development in social marketing, whether it is your full-time focus or one of several responsibilities. Social marketing is a developing field, and there is always more to learn. Seeking opportunities for further training, reading, or discussion with others can help keep you energized about your work, and ensure that you are a resource for those to whom you are promoting social marketing.
- Think like a marketer–Regardless of what tasks and activities you undertake, approach the promotion of social marketing with a marketing mind-set:

  - Think behavior change
  - Know your audience
  - Think costs and benefits of behavior
  - When and where is the audience in the right frame of mind?
  - When and where is the right place and time to intervene?

An additional lesson is that learning is a continuous process. DPH's experience has shown that there is always more to learn about how to use a social marketing approach, regardless of the stage of change or the experience of the practitioner. Rather than a learning curve, it may be useful to think of one's development as a social marketer as a spiral. Thus, even when one is in the action or maintenance phase of the stages of change, one can always go higher (or deeper) into the scholarship and practice of the social marketing approach. As a logistical consideration when planning interventions, remember that they most likely will need to be repeated. Recurring exposure to educational offerings and case studies of social marketing applications cement concepts for the audience, and help reinforce their sense of self-efficacy and a belief that social marketing is effective.

Another lesson is that different individuals and programs in a complex organization move through the stages of change at different rates. Be prepared for the possibility of having multiple interventions targeting various audiences occurring at the same time. If this stresses your resources, select one or two audiences that will have the greatest effect on promoting social marketing in the organization and work solely with them. Make a conscious decision to work only with the director's office, or only with program staff who are in the contemplation stage, for example. However, be prepared in the event that as you successfully market social marketing with one audience, others may want to come on board, thus making additional demands on your resources.

REFERENCES

Andreasen, Alan (1995), *Marketing Social Change,* San Francisco: Jossey-Bass.

———— (2002), "Marketing Social Marketing in the Social Change Marketplace," *Journal Of Public Policy and Marketing, 21*(1), 3-13.

Basil, Michael (2000), "Managerial and Strategic Approaches to Establishing a Marketing Orientation in Social Change Organizations," *Social Marketing Quarterly,* VI (3), 18-19.

Bryant, Carol (1997), "Social Marketing–A Tool for Excellence," paper presented at the Seventh Annual Social Marketing in Public Health Conference, Clearwater Beach, FL.

Dearing, James W. (2004), "Improving the State of Health Programming by Using Diffusion Theory," *Journal Of Health Communication, 9*(Suppl 1), 21-36.

Donovan, Robert and Nadine Henley (2003), *Social Marketing Principles and Practices,* Melbourne, Australia: IP Communications.

Fishbein, Martin, Harry C. Triandis, Frederick H. Kanfer, Marshall Becker, Susan E. Middlestadt, and Anita Eichler (2001), "Factors Influencing Behavior And Behavior Change," in *Handbook Of Health Psychology*, ed. Andrew Baum, Tracy A. Revenson, and Jerome. E. Singer, Mahwah, NJ: Lawrence Erlbaum, 3-17.

Kotler, Philip, Ned Roberto, and Nancy Lee (2002), *Social Marketing: Improving the Quality of Life,* Thousand Oaks, CA: Sage.

Kutz, Martha (2000), "Social Marketing in CDC's Toolkit," *Social Marketing Quarterly,* VI (3), 22-24.

Maibach, Edward (2000), "Five Strategies for Encouraging a Marketing Orientation in Social Change Organizations," *Social Marketing Quarterly,* VI (3), 25-26.

Maibach, Edward and David Cotton (1995), "Moving People to Behavior Change: A Staged Social Cognitive Approach to Message Design," in *Designing Health Messages*, ed. Edward Maibach and Roxanne L. Parrott, Newbury Park, CA: Sage Publications, 41–64.

Middlestadt, Susan E., Karabi Bhattacharyya, Julia Rosenbaum, Martin Fishbein, and Melissa Shepherd (1996), "The Use of Theory Based Semistructured Elicitation Questionnaires: Formative Research for CDC's Prevention Marketing Initiative," *Public Health Reports,* III, Supplement I, 18-27.

Newton-Ward, Mike (2004), "Building Social Marketeering Capacity at the State Level: North Carolina's Social Marketing Matrix Team," *The Health Education Monograph Series, 21*(1), 25-29.

Prochaska, James O. and Carlo C. DiClemente (1983), "Stages and Processes of Self-Change in Smoking: Toward an Integrative Model of Change," *Journal Of Consulting and Clinical Psychology, 51*(31), 390-95.

Prochaska, James O., Colleen A. Redding, and Kerry E. Evers (2002), "The Trans-theoretical Model and Stages of Change," in *Health Behavior and Health Education: Theory, Research, and Practice*, ed. Karen Glanz, Barbara K. Rimer, and Frances M. Lewis, San Francisco: Jossey-Bass, 99-120.

Steckler, Allen, Robert M. Goodman, and Michelle Crozier Kegler (2002), "Mobilizing Organizations for Health Enhancement: Theories of Organizational Change," in *Health Behavior and Health Education: Theory, Research, and Practice*, ed. Karen Glanz, Barbara K. Rimer, and Frances M. Lewis, San Francisco: Jossey-Bass, 35-360.

Smith, William (1999), "Marketing With No Budget," *Social Marketing Quarterly*, V (2), 6-11.

Strand, John and Yalonda Lewis (2003), "Doing Better at Doing Good: Adding a Competitive Perspective," paper presented at the Thirteenth Annual Social Marketing in Public Health Conference, Clearwater Beach, FL.

Turning Point Social Marketing National Excellence Collaborative (2000), "Mission," http://www.turningpointprogram.org/Pages/socialmkt.html.

Turning Point Social Marketing Collaborative, U.S. Centers for Disease Control and Prevention, and Academy for Educational Development (2003), "CDCynergy: Social Marketing Edition" (Beta Version)[Computer software], Atlanta, GA: CDC Office of Communication.

doi:10.1300/J054v17n01_03

EMPIRICAL ARTICLES

The Response to the Commitment with Block-Leader Recycling Promotion Technique: A Longitudinal Approach

Gonzalo Díaz Meneses
Asunción Beerli Palacio

SUMMARY. This article focuses on the study of the changes in consumers' recycling beliefs, attitudes, and behavior due to the application of one promotion technique: a commitment by block leader technique characterized by the agreeing participant signing a request or statement in which s/he makes a commitment to recycle as a result of the encouragement of a person who belongs to the same social circle. We therefore

Gonzalo Díaz Meneses is Ph Lecturer, Universidad de Las Palmas de Gran Canaria, Facultad de Ciencias Económicas y Empresariales, Módulo C, despacho 1.02, 35017 Campus de Tafira, The Canary Islands (SPAIN) (E-mail: gdiaz@dede.ulpgc.es).

Asunción Beerli Palacio is Professor, Universidad de Las Palmas de Gran Canaria, Facultad de Ciencias Económicas y Empresariales, Módulo C, despacho 1.06, 35017 Campus de Tafira, The Canary Islands (SPAIN) (E-mail: abeerli@dede.ulpgc.es).

[Haworth co-indexing entry note]: "The Response to the Commitment with Block-Leader Recycling Promotion Technique: A Longitudinal Approach." Meneses, Gonzalo Díaz, and Asunción Beerli Palacio. Co-published simultaneously in *Journal of Nonprofit & Public Sector Marketing* (Best Business Books, an imprint of The Haworth Press, Inc.) Vol. 17, No. 1/2, 2007, pp. 83-102; and: *Social Marketing: Advances in Research and Theory* (eds: Debra Z. Basil and Walter Wymer) Best Business Books, an imprint of The Haworth Press, Inc., 2007, pp. 83-102. Single or multiple copies of this article are available for a fee from The Haworth Document Delivery Service [1-800-HAWORTH, 9:00 a.m. - 5:00 p.m. (EST). E-mail address: docdelivery@haworthpress.com].

Available online at http://jnpsm.haworthpress.com
doi:10.1300/J054v17n01_04

carried out a quasi-experimental work whose results enable us to explain the response to this recycling promotion technique. It makes a contribution to existing environmental literature by (1) systemizing the set of existing doctrines in order to explain the response to this recycling promotion technique, and (2) revealing the effects of this technique on people's beliefs and attitudes. The practical implications that may stem from these contributions are of an educational nature and should be of use to the public management of promotion campaigns. doi:10.1300/

J054v17n01_04 *[Article copies available for a fee from The Haworth Document Delivery Service: 1-800-HAWORTH. E-mail address: <docdelivery@haworth-press.com> Website: <http://www.HaworthPress.com> © 2007 by The Haworth Press, Inc. All rights reserved.]*

KEYWORDS. Environmental cognitions and attitudes, recycling behavior, green promotion techniques, social marketing

INTRODUCTION

There has still not been sufficient research carried out to explain the changes in consumers' recycling beliefs, attitudes and behavior due to the application of promotion techniques (Hopper and Nielsen, 1991; Leeming et al., 1993; Shrum et al., 1994; Wesley et al., 1995), aimed at exploring the alternatives that give rise to maximum receptiveness and response (Vining and Ebreo, 1989). Some of these recycling promotion techniques are commitment and the block leader, which are usually jointly applied because this combination is very effective in encouraging the desired responses (Bryce, Day, and Olney, 1997; Burn and Oskamp, 1986; Deleon and Fuqua, 1995; Folz, 1991; Hamad et al., 1980; Hopper and Nielsen, 1991; Katzev and Pardini, 1987; McCaul and Kopp, 1982; Pardini and Katzev, 1983; Wan and Katzev, 1990).

The objective of this research is to explain the different ways of encouraging and strengthening recycling behavior, in order to analyze empirically the immediate and sustained effectiveness of one particular recycling promotion technique: the technique of commitment with a block leader. In order to achieve the desired goal, this work is structured in four parts: (1) a review of existing literature, in which the diverse hypotheses are set out; (2) the methodological process; (3) an analysis of the empirical results, which includes an examination of the reliability and validity of the measuring instruments used, as well as a study of the results relating to the longitudinal effects of this recycling promotion technique; and, finally, (4) the conclusions in order to synthesize the results, the academic and professional implications, the limitations and future lines of research.

REVIEW OF EXISTING LITERATURE

The technique of commitment by block-leader encouragement is characterized by the participant signing a request or statement in which he/she promises to recycle (Dwyer et al., 1993; Geller, 1989; Geller, Chaffee, and Ingram, 1975; Hutton and Markley, 1991) as a result of the encouragement of a person who acts as persuader and who belongs to the same social circle (Burn, 1991; McKenzie-Mohr, 1999). In this work, the block leader is a member of the household who already engages in the behavior being promoted and has agreed to speak to other members of the household to help them get started. This block leader uses a written and individual commitment that is given to other members of the household to be signed.

The effectiveness of this type of technique is studied using the framework of attitude models as the starting point. Following Lutz (1991), we have based ourselves theoretically on the uni-dimensional acceptance of attitude that is identified with people's evaluations, and which, in contrast to tripartite orientation, transfers people's beliefs and intentions or conduct outside the notion of attitude. Taking existing environmental literature as a basis, we distinguish the following as cognitive components: (1) ecological conscience (Arcury, Johnson, and Scollay, 1986; Bigné, 1997), and (2) beliefs about recycling (Bagozzi and Dabholkar, 1994; Wesley, Oskamp, and Mainieri, 1995). The evaluations and attitudes used in this research are: (1) ecological concern (Bohlen, Schlegelmilch, and Diamantopoulos, 1993; Grunert and Jorn, 1995; Zimmer, Stafford, and Royne, 1994); (2) involvement with recycling (Alwitt and Pitts, 1996; Black, Stern, and Elworth, 1985; McGuiness, Jones, and Cole, 1977; Oskamp et al., 1991; Peatty, 1990; Simmons and Widmar, 1990), and (3) attitude toward recycling (Hornik et al., 1995; Oskamp et al., 1991).

We would like to explain the internal and external consistency principles in order to base the incentive effect on a doctrine. In theory and following the internal consistency explanation, cognitions, evaluations, and behaviors tend to maintain the same direction, and so conflicts among such components are thus avoided because this balance explains the maintenance of the desired response. From an external perspective and based on the social or external consistency principle, evaluations and beliefs are not in themselves sufficient to predict the behavior, since an additional element, the subjective norm effect, influences the final response. This can happen because of two different effects: (1) people make their cognitions, attitudes, and behaviors by considering social pressure or the effects of what people believe other people think they should do, and (2) attitudes performing a value-expressive function express the consumer's central values or self-concept and state that s/he is a person with a social identity. The internal and external consistency principles coincide in stating that the transformation of beliefs and evaluations guarantees the development and maintenance of the desired behavior.

The predominant paradigm in the recycling literature to explain the response, applying the consistency principles to this kind of technique, is the theory of multiple attributes (Fishbein, 1963) and of reasoned action (Azjen and Fishbein, 1977). According to these frameworks, consumers approach recycling conduct by first accumulating knowledge and then by forming their attitudes. This is also evident in relatively recent works (Biswas et al., 2000; Emmet, 1990). Nevertheless, in many cases, this hierarchy of effects based on the Fishbein models are used in ways that may not warrant certain assumptions about recycling behavior. For example: (1) no works have been found with the aim of contradicting the classic hierarchy of effects related to this high-commitment paradigm; (2) much evidence points to the existence of associations or correlations, and not of cause-and-effect relationships or a longitudinal approach (Schlegelmich et al., 1996), and (3) some works make it clear that the public's interpretation of environmental guidelines might be not only intentional, for instance, a routine (Chan and Lau, 2000; Vining and Ebreo, 1989; Vining and Ebreo, 1990; Williams, 1991), but also an emotional response to frequent environmental campaigns (Ratneshwar, Glen, and Huffman, 2003). Therefore, the classic hierarchy of effects might not be the only theoretical framework on which to base the consistency principle.

In fact, in line with Andreasen (1995), there are two consumer-behavior constructs that are valuable in understanding the maintenance of the desired conduct from a consistency cognitive approach. One is the cognitive dissonance theory; the other is the behavior modification doctrine. The cognitive dissonance theory stresses the idea that individuals seek to maximize some psychological consistency between their cognitions and behaviors since inconsistency is taken to be an uncomfortable state, and hence individuals strive to avoid it. Therefore, it is said to be a post-decisional phenomenon since dissonance occurs after the decision has been made and the behavior adopted. Based on this theoretical framework, block-leader influence is understood as provoking a dissonance effect, not only by providing information and using subjective norms, but also by inducing commitment to the desired behavior.

In addition, it may be useful to mention that there are a number of alternatives to the cognitive dissonance theory that emphasize the centrality of the concept of self to contradictory phenomena. For example, according to Aronson (1999) dissonance most easily stems from inconsistencies that specifically involve the self and a part of behavior that violates that self-concept. In this sense, the induced compliance commitment to recycling may involve an inconsistency with one's actual behavior and so set in motion a process designed to restore consistency between the commitment and the promised conduct. Another view that also emphasizes the centrality of self is the self-affirmation theory (Steel, 1988). This theory points out the importance of maintaining an image of the self as competent, coherent, and morally adequate; in other words, with some perception of self-integrity. Both approaches coincide in pointing out processes that are activated by information sourced from the internal sphere. Furthermore, the cognitive dissonance mechanism may come about from the external sphere. In this sense, the block leader shows a direct influence on the consumer's own perceptions of specific environmental consequences of recycling behavior. In fact, as block leader and target both belong to the same social circle they tend to share the same values and attitudes toward the crucial things (Spaccarelli, Zolik, and Jason, 1989).

The other approach consists of the behavior modification doctrines, which argue that much behavior is influenced by environmental factors that appear both before the desired conduct (for example, block leader interventions) and after (for example, the satisfaction of accomplishing the commitment). In this context and according to the doctrine of instrumental learning (Carey et al., 1976), commitment and block leader are non-conditional stimuli that, after being associated with the appearance of the desired response, serve to reinforce it, up to the point that, if the stimuli are withdrawn, a continued recycling behavior becomes more probable. Moreover, from a behaviorist psychology literature perspective, commitment and block leader provide positive contingency by the social pressure and information that will make that behavior more frequent. In short, behavioral theorists urge social marketers to pay close attention to the rewards that can follow behavior (Andreasen, 1995).

Perhaps most dissonance theory and behavior modification doctrine inspired research concerning what is commonly called induced compliance. Induced compliance is said to occur when an individual is induced to act in a way contrary to his or her beliefs and attitudes, for instance, to advocate some viewpoint opposed to his/her position (O'Keefe, 2002). However, according to Kok and Siero (1985), it does not appear logical that block leader and commitment are especially suitable for people rejecting recycling but are for those who are merely not opposed or favorable. In fact, O'Keefe (2002) points out that sometimes a persuader's task is not so much to encourage people to have the desired attitudes as it is to encourage people to act on existing attitudes. For example, people commonly express positive attitudes toward recycling but fail to act accordingly. Based on the hypocrisy induction mechanisms, presumably the underlying mechanism arising from the commitment by means of a block leader involves the salience of attitude behavior inconsistency. Applying this theory to the recycling context, the basic idea is that a block leader can call attention to the inconsistency of a person's attitudes and actions. This individual's hypocrisy can arouse dissonance, which is then reduced through behavioral change. Thus adopting recycling behavior, the individual makes his/her desired conduct consistent with the existing attitude. Hence, both the cognitive dissonance and the behavior modification doctrines not only justify a process of adoption in line with the consistency principles, they also explain the change in beliefs and attitudes in accordance with the indirect effects that result from the prior appearance of the behavior.

In existing environmental literature, the explanation of the maintenance of recycling behavior has been purely theoretical, with no empirical studies having been carried out to date. Based on the consistency principle, several recycling works explain why both kinds of techniques achieve the desired and sustained behavior. With respect to the commitment technique, it states that it stimulates the internal behavioral control forming part of the intrinsic process of individual consistency motivation (Dwyer et al., 1993; Katzev and Pardini, 1987; McKenzie-Mohr, 1999; Wesley et al., 1995). It also drives the subject to the verge of collaborative conduct and activates the self-congruence mechanism (Burn, 1991; McKenzie-Mohr, 1999; Pardini and Katzev, 1983). From an external perspective and with reference to the block-leader technique, it seems clear that public inconsistency is very badly regarded and there is no doubt about the fact that recycling is a good act (Minton and Rose,

1997). There are various explanations to understand and define social influence: Pardini and Katzev (1983) and Wesley et al. (1995) refer to the need for social recognition and approval and, according to Hopper and Nielsen (1991), the desired conduct appears by the natural principle of imitation. In short, the block-leader and commitment techniques act by means of social influence and the provision of information (Bagozzi and Dabholkar, 1994; Hopper and Nielsen, 1991), in other words, by means of social or internal consistency principles.

Both the commitment technique and the block-leader technique are recycling promotions that show good results because they maintain the response even after the stimulus is withdrawn. This has been corroborated in several works about both the commitment technique (Bryce et al., 1997; Katzev and Pardini, 1987; Pardini and Katzev, 1983; Wan and Katzev, 1990) and the block-leader technique (Hamad et al., 1980; Hopper and Nielsen, 1991).

Thus, considering these empirical results and the internal and external consistency principles explained by the cognitive dissonance theory and the behavior modification doctrine, we predict that the commitment and block-leader technique will provoke changes in ecological and recycling components, both cognitive and evaluative, so that the recycling behavior is sustained. Along these lines, a set of six hypotheses are proposed:

H1: *The immediate and sustained responses to the technique of commitment with block leader consist of an increase in the consumer's ecological conscience.*

H2: *The immediate and sustained responses to the technique of commitment with block leader consist of an increase in the consumer's recycling beliefs.*

H3: *The immediate and sustained responses to the technique of commitment with block leader consist of an increase in the consumer's ecological concern.*

H4: *The immediate and sustained responses to the technique of commitment with block leader consist of an increase in the consumer's attitude toward recycling.*

H5: *The immediate and sustained responses to the technique of commitment with block leader consist of an increase in the consumer's recycling involvement.*

H6: *The immediate and sustained responses to the technique of commitment with block leader consist of an increase in the consumer's recycling behavior.*

METHODOLOGICAL ASPECTS

In order to analyze empirically the immediate and sustained effectiveness of the technique of commitment with a block leader, a quasi-experimental design was developed that is characterized by being performed in natural settings and with conveniently constituted groups (Moreno and López, 1985). Thus, this recycling promotion technique is considered as an independent variable and the ecological conscience, beliefs about recycling, ecological concern, involvement with recycling, attitude toward recycling, and recycling behavior as dependent variables.

The treatment designed consists of the application of the technique of written and individual commitment at the encouragement of a block leader. The written commitment is worded as follows: "I, the undersigned, wish to recycle glass, paper, and cardboard in order to assist the municipal selective waste program." We have a large team of block leaders comprising a total of 123 volunteers, enrolled from students in our business-college center, who each selected one member of their respective households as an experimental participant. Thus each volunteer was responsible for applying the treatment to that selected member of their household.

In order to gather the information related to dependent variables, the authors designed a questionnaire that was issued three times and gathered information about the participant's ecological and recycling beliefs and attitudes, as well as their recycling behavior. The scales used to measure these ecological and recycling components are shown in Table 1. Although all the information was gathered by a survey, the authors were able to control whether there had been important differences between the indirect measurement gathered by questionnaires and the direct measurements made by our contacted volunteers.

Table 2 shows the chronogram of the experiment, which lasted almost three months although the promotion period was little more than one week. Once the information had been gathered it was introduced into the database and processed, eliminating any cases displaying internal incoherence, where the object of the research had been discovered by the individual being surveyed and where the individual had stopped participating in the longitudinal study. After eliminating 30 entries, the real sample comprised 193 individuals, 123 of whom were assigned to the treatment of subscribing to commitment by block-leader encouragement. In order to ensure the internal validity of the experiment, a control group was formed of 70 individuals who were not subjected to any treatment or promotion.

TABLE 1. Characteristics of the Scales Referring to the Cognitive and Evaluation Components

Dependent variables or factors	Scale and references	Items
Ecological conscience	*Likert* 4 *items* and 5 points. Bohlen et al. (1993)	I know what the main ecological problems are.
		In general, I know how not to damage the ecosystem.
		I sufficiently understand what is said about the deterioration of nature.
		In general, I can distinguish what is bad and what is good for the natural environment.
Beliefs about recycling	*Likert* 6 *items* and 5 points. Scholder (1994)	I know how to recycle.
		I know more about recycling than the average person.
		I know what materials can be recycled.
		I know the reasons why recycling is promoted.
Involvement with recycling	Semantic differential, 4 *items*, 5 points. Zaichkowsky (1985); Díaz y Beerli (2002)	It means nothing to me / It means a lot to me
		It is not in my interest /It is in my interest
		I am not interested / I am interested
		It is not my responsibility / It is my responsibility
Attitude toward recycling	Likert, 4 *items*, 5 points Biswas et al. (1990); Shrum et al. (1994)	Recycling is Bad / Good
		Recycling is Stupid / Wise
		Recycling is Undesirable / Desirable
		Recycling is Not valuable /Very valuable
Ecological concern	*Likert*, 4 *items*, five points. Biswas et al. (2000); Shrum et al. (1994)	When man interferes with nature, it often leads to disastrous consequences.
		Mankind is severely abusing the environment.
		The balance of nature is very delicate and can change very easily.
		If things continue as they are, we will experience a great ecological catastrophe.

As each our volunteers belonged to the same household or social network of each surveyed, this procedure consisted of using samples of convenience. In this case, the convenience samples are defensible because there is greater opportunity for observation and control of the individuals in the experiment.

The recycling materials chosen for this research are: glass, *paper*, and cardboard, and cardboard, metal or plastic containers.

TABLE 2. Program of Activities

Month		Activities	Month		Activities	Month		Activities
October			November			December		
Tuesday	1		Friday	1		Sunday	1	
Wednesday	2		Saturday	2		Monday	2	
Thursday	3		Sunday	3		Tuesday	3	
Friday	4		Monday	4	TIME 2=T2	Wednesday	4	
Saturday	5		Tuesday	5	Duration of the second issue of questionnaire and their return to the research director ("b" question-naire).	Thursday	5	
Sunday	6		Wednesday	6		Friday	6	
Monday	7	TIME 1=T1	Thursday	7		Saturday	7	
Tuesday	8	Duration of the first issue of questionnaires and their return to the research director ("a" and "b" questionnaires).	Friday	8		Sunday	8	
Wednesday	9		Saturday	9		Monday	9	TIME 3=T3
Thursday	10		Sunday	10		Tuesday	10	Duration of the third issue of questionnaire and their return to the research director ("b" questionnaire).
Friday	11		Monday	11		Wednesday	11	
Saturday	12		Tuesday	12	Data base processing.	Thursday	12	
Sunday	13		Wednesday	13		Friday	13	
Monday	14		Thursday	14		Saturday	14	
Tuesday	15	Database processing.	Friday	15		Sunday	15	
Wednesday	16		Saturday	16		Monday	16	
Thursday	17		Sunday	17		Tuesday	17	Data base processing.
Friday	18		Monday	18		Wednesday	18	
Saturday	19		Tuesday	19		Thursday	19	
Sunday	20		Wednesday	20		Friday	20	
Monday	21	Duration of the promotion: Commitment with block leader.	Thursday	21		Saturday	21	
Tuesday	22		Friday	22		Sunday	22	
Wednesday	23		Saturday	23		Monday	23	
Thursday	24		Sunday	24		Tuesday	24	
Friday	25		Monday	25		Wednesday	25	
Saturday	26		Tuesday	26		Thursday	26	
Sunday	27		Wednesday	27		Friday	27	
Monday	28		Thursday	28		Saturday	28	
Tuesday	29		Friday	29		Sunday	29	
Wednesday	30		Saturday	30		Monday	30	
Thursday	31					Tuesday	31	

ANALYSIS OF RESULTS

Preliminaries

Prior to testing the hypotheses, the validity and reliability of the measuring instruments was checked by means of exploratory factorial, Cronbach's alpha, and confirmatory factorial analyses on the cognitive components and the evaluation, ecological, and recycling components. The exploratory factorial analysis with varimax rotation identified all the ecological and recycling characteristics under consideration and explained over 60% of variance, except in the case of ecological concern, with values of around 50%.

After the exploratory factorial analyses, a confirmatory factorial analysis was run in order to check the convergent validity of the same scales. The measuring instruments showed a good fit to the data, and the indicators produced adequate results for the five cognitive, ecological character evaluations and recycling characteristic variables. The standardized estimators are significant and positive, with values of over 0.5 in all cases except in the scale referring to ecological concern, with a value of 0.4. To study the reliability, an analysis of construct reliability and extracted variance was carried out, together with Cronbach's alpha. All the measurements obtained were above the recommended threshold, except for the extracted variance of ecological concern, which was below that value. Consequently, it can be said that the scales for ecological conscience, recycling beliefs, recycling attitude, and involvement showed values that indicate the reliability of the dimensions under consideration, while the scale for ecological concern was close to the critical threshold of 0.40. Lastly, in order to check the discriminatory validity of the measuring instruments, a correlations analysis was made, which showed that ecological conscience, recycling beliefs, ecological concern, recycling attitude, and recycling involvement measure different ecological and recycling realities, with Pearson's correlation coefficient well below the value of 1.

Analysis to Contrast Hypothesis

Before studying the effectiveness of the commitment with blockleader technique, a student t-test of independent samples at moment t1 between the control and the experimental group was carried out. This was aimed at checking whether there are any statistically significant differences between these variables before the application of the promotion technique. On the basis of the results obtained, it can be concluded that no statistically significant differences exist between the groups regarding the cognitive components and the evaluation and behavior components at moment t1, or before the promotion was applied.

In order to explore the evolution of the ecological and recycling components related to hypotheses 1 and 2, a student t-test of related samples was first used to identify the intensity, direction and permanence of the changes in beliefs and evaluations, as well as in recycling conduct due to the application of the commitment with block-leader promotion technique. Beliefs about recycling and behavior increased immediately after the application of the promotion and were maintained at t3. One month after the end of the promotion, in addition to beliefs and behavior, recycling involvement, recycling attitude, and ecological conscience increased significantly.

Finally, it is necessary to compare the immediate and the sustained evolution of ecological and recycling components in both sub-samples considering the moderating role of some variables in order to be able to conclude whether the hypotheses are confirmed. Therefore, in order to test this, an analysis based on the General Linear Model (GLM) of repeated measures was carried out that determined the differential norms of evolution of the ecological and recycling variables under consideration.

Finally, including these variables in the GLM analysis, it can be stated that there are statistically significant differences in beliefs about recycling and recycling behavior in the short term (tables 4 and 8) and in ecological conscience, beliefs about recycling, recycling attitude, and recycling behavior (tables 3, 5, 6, and 7) in the long term. This means that the commitment with block-leader technique has a great capacity for long-term maintenance of these components and this is due to the appearance of the behavior prior to the later evolution of the cognitive and evaluative components. However, there are no statistically significant differences in terms of ecological conscience and concern, recycling attitudes and involvement with recycling immediately after the application of the promotions.

On the basis of the above, it can be concluded that hypothesis 1 is supported because ecological conscience changed due to the sustained effect of commitment encouraged by a block leader. However, the two sub-samples show no statistically significant differences in ecological conscience in the short term.

Hypothesis 2, which proposes that "the immediate and sustained responses to the technique of commitment with block leader consist of an

TABLE 3. General Linear Model of Repeated Measures Analysis on Ecological Conscience to Contrast Hypothesis 1

			Value	F	LG hypothesis	LG error	Significance
Immediate T1-T2	Evolution	Pillai	0.001	0.253	1.000	191.000	0.616
		Wilks	0.999	0.253	1.000	191.000	0.616
		Hotelling	0.001	0.253	1.000	191.000	0.616
		Roy	0.001	0.253	1.000	191.000	0.616
	Comparing evolution	Pillai	0.014	2.703	1.000	191.000	0.102
		Wilks	0.986	2.703	1.000	191.000	0.102
		Hotelling	0.014	2.703	1.000	191.000	0.102
		Roy	0.014	2.703	1.000	191.000	0.102
	Error	Square Sum: 113.994; LG: 191; Square Mean: 0.597					
Sustained T1-T3	Evolution	Pillai	0.000	0.002	1.000	191.000	0.968
		Wilks	1.000	0.002	1.000	191.000	0.968
		Hotelling	0.000	0.002	1.000	191.000	0.968
		Roy	0.000	0.002	1.000	191.000	0.968
	Comparing evolution	Pillai	0.021	4.161	1.000	191.000	0.043
		Wilks	0.979	4.161	1.000	191.000	0.043
		Hotelling	0.022	4.161	1.000	191.000	0.043
		Roy	0.022	4.161	1.000	191.000	0.043
	Error	Square Sum: 106.365; LG: 191; Square Mean: 0.557					

TABLE 4. General Linear Model of Repeated Measures Analysis on Beliefs About Recycling to Contrast Hypothesis 2

			Value	F	LG hypothesis	LG error	Significance
Immediate T1-T2	Evolution	Pillai	0.000	0.028	1.000	191.000	0.868
		Wilks	1.000	0.028	1.000	191.000	0.868
		Hotelling	0.000	0.028	1.000	191.000	0.868
		Roy	0.000	0.028	1.000	191.000	0.868
	Comparing evolution	Pillai	0.029	5.708	1.000	191.000	0.018
		Wilks	0.971	5.708	1.000	191.000	0.018
		Hotelling	0.030	5.708	1.000	191.000	0.018
		Roy	0.030	5.708	1.000	191.000	0.018
	Error	Square Sum: 87.215; LG: 191; Square Mean: 0.457					
Sustained T1-T3	Evolution	Pillai	0.000	0.003	1.000	191.000	0.957
		Wilks	1.000	0.003	1.000	191.000	0.957
		Hotelling	0.000	0.003	1.000	191.000	0.957
		Roy	0.000	0.003	1.000	191.000	0.957
	Comparing evolution	Pillai	0.033	6.616	1.000	191.000	0.011
		Wilks	0.967	6.616	1.000	191.000	0.011
		Hotelling	0.035	6.616	1.000	191.000	0.011
		Roy	0.035	6.616	1.000	191.000	0.011
	Error	Square Sum: 97.218; LG: 191; Square Mean: 0.509					

TABLE 5. General Linear Model of Repeated Measures Analysis on Ecological Concern to Contrast Hypothesis 3

			Value	F	LG hypothesis	LG error	Significance
Immediate T1-T2	Evolution	Pillai	0.003	0.664	1.000	191.000	0.416
		Wilks	0.997	0.664	1.000	191.000	0.416
		Hotelling	0.003	0.664	1.000	191.000	0.416
		Roy	0.003	0.664	1.000	191.000	0.416
	Comparing evolution	Pillai	0.006	1.089	1.000	191.000	0.298
		Wilks	0.994	1.089	1.000	191.000	0.298
		Hotelling	0.006	1.089	1.000	191.000	0.298
		Roy	0.006	1.089	1.000	191.000	0.298
	Error		Square Sum: 90.458; LG: 191; Square Mean: 0.474				
Sustained T1-T3	Evolution	Pillai	0.000	0.007	1.000	191.000	0.936
		Wilks	1.000	0.007	1.000	191.000	0.936
		Hotelling	0.000	0.007	1.000	191.000	0.936
		Roy	0.000	0.007	1.000	191.000	0.936
	Comparing evolution	Pillai	0.005	0.864	1.000	191.000	0.354
		Wilks	0.995	0.864	1.000	191.000	0.354
		Hotelling	0.005	0.864	1.000	191.000	0.354
		Roy	0.005	0.864	1.000	191.000	0.354
	Error		Square Sum: 107.945; LG: 191; Square Mean: 0.565				

TABLE 6. General Linear Model of Repeated Measures Analysis on Attitude Toward Recycling to Contrast Hypothesis 4

			Value	F	LG hypothesis	LG error	Significance
Immediate T1-T2	Evolution	Pillai	0.001	0.241	1.000	191.000	0.624
		Wilks	0.999	0.241	1.000	191.000	0.624
		Hotelling	0.001	0.241	1.000	191.000	0.624
		Roy	0.001	0.241	1.000	191.000	0.624
	Comparing evolution	Pillai	0.003	0.615	1.000	191.000	0.434
		Wilks	0.997	0.615	1.000	191.000	0.434
		Hotelling	0.003	0.615	1.000	191.000	0.434
		Roy	0.003	0.615	1.000	191.000	0.434
	Error		Square Sum: 56.888; LG: 191; Square Mean: 0.298				
Sustained T1-T3	Evolution	Pillai	0.001	0.251	1.000	191.000	0.617
		Wilks	0.999	0.251	1.000	191.000	0.617
		Hotelling	0.001	0.251	1.000	191.000	0.617
		Roy	0.001	0.251	1.000	191.000	0.617
	Comparing evolution	Pillai	0.051	10.176	1.000	191.000	0.002
		Wilks	0.949	10.176	1.000	191.000	0.002
		Hotelling	0.053	10.176	1.000	191.000	0.002
		Roy	0.053	10.176	1.000	191.000	0.002
	Error		Square Sum: 65.640; LG: 191; Square Mean: 0.344				

TABLE 7. General Linear Model of Repeated Measures Analysis on Involvement with Recycling to Contrast Hypothesis 5

			Value	F	LG hypothesis	LG error	Significance
Immediate T1-T2	Evolution	Pillai	0.007	1.431	1.000	191.000	0.233
		Wilks	0.993	1.431	1.000	191.000	0.233
		Hotelling	0.007	1.431	1.000	191.000	0.233
		Roy	0.007	1.431	1.000	191.000	0.233
	Comparing evolution	Pillai	0.009	1.677	1.000	191.000	0.197
		Wilks	0.991	1.677	1.000	191.000	0.197
		Hotelling	0.009	1.677	1.000	191.000	0.197
		Roy	0.009	1.677	1.000	191.000	0.197
	Error		Square Sum: 52.624; LG: 191; Square Mean: 0.276				
Sustained T1-T3	Evolution	Pillai	0.008	1.608	1.000	191.000	0.206
		Wilks	0.992	1.608	1.000	191.000	0.206
		Hotelling	0.008	1.608	1.000	191.000	0.206
		Roy	0.008	1.608	1.000	191.000	0.206
	Comparing evolution	Pillai	0.021	4.036	1.000	191.000	0.046
		Wilks	0.979	4.036	1.000	191.000	0.046
		Hotelling	0.021	4.036	1.000	191.000	0.046
		Roy	0.021	4.036	1.000	191.000	0.046
	Error		Square Sum: 57.706; LG: 191; Square Mean: 0.302				

TABLE 8. General Linear Model of Repeated Measures Analysis on Recycling Behavior to Contrast Hypothesis 6

			Value	F	LG hypothesis	LG error	Significance
Immediate T1-T2	Evolution	Pillai	0.131	28.719	1.000	191.000	0.000
		Wilks	0.869	28.719	1.000	191.000	0.000
		Hotelling	0.150	28.719	1.000	191.000	0.000
		Roy	0.150	28.719	1.000	191.000	0.000
	Comparing evolution	Pillai	0.045	8.902	1.000	191.000	0.003
		Wilks	0.955	8.902	1.000	191.000	0.003
		Hotelling	0.047	8.902	1.000	191.000	0.003
		Roy	0.047	8.902	1.000	191.000	0.003
	Error		Square Sum: 83.899; LG: 191; Square Mean: 0.439				
Sustained T1-T3	Evolution	Pillai	0.133	29.190	1.000	191.000	0.000
		Wilks	0.867	29.190	1.000	191.000	0.000
		Hotelling	0.153	29.190	1.000	191.000	0.000
		Roy	0.153	29.190	1.000	191.000	0.000
	Comparing evolution	Pillai	0.058	11.811	1.000	191.000	0.001
		Wilks	0.942	11.811	1.000	191.000	0.001
		Hotelling	0.062	11.811	1.000	191.000	0.001
		Roy	0.062	11.811	1.000	191.000	0.001
	Error		Square Sum: 89.971; LG: 191; Square Mean: 0.471				

increase in the consumer's recycling beliefs," is supported because recycling beliefs changed markedly due to the effect of the promotion.

By contrast, hypothesis 3 is rejected since there was not any significant change in ecological concern after the promotion was applied.

Similarly, hypotheses 4 and 5 are supported. This is because the sustained responses to the promotion consisted of an increase in the consumer's recycling attitude and involvement, although this evolution occurs in the long term.

Finally, as the immediate and sustained responses to the technique of commitment with block leader consisted of an increase in the consumer's recycling behavior, hypothesis 6 is supported.

CONCLUSIONS

Based on the results of the present research, we can conclude that the immediate response to the commitment encouraged by a block-leader technique is not characterized by an immediate change in the attitudinal components. It has been demonstrated that recycling beliefs and recycling behavior represent the only possibility of people responding to this promotion technique in the short term. Furthermore, with reference to sustained effectiveness, the individuals who maintain their recycling collaboration respond according to changes in ecological and recycling, cognitive, and attitudinal components. In short, the first model of response corresponds to the sequence of behavior adoption characterized by a cognitive dissonance (Festinger and Carlsmith, 1959) whose evolution leads to a more ecological and attitudinal based behavior with time. Therefore it is clear that the technique of commitment by group-leader encouragement shows high levels of effectiveness in the long term.

Further theoretical justification to explain the success of programs based on commitments and block leader to sustain recycling behavior is that proposed by the doctrine of behavioral modification. As it was mentioned above, both cognitive dissonance and behavioral modification theories not only justify a process of adoption other than that of the consistency principles, but also explain the change in beliefs and attitudes in accordance with the indirect effects that result from the previous appearance of the behavior. In conclusion, our results lead us to point out that the classic hierarchy of effects is not the best theoretical framework upon which to base the consistency principle and to explain the immediate response to this kind of technique, although the theories of multiple attributes (Fishbein, 1963) and reasoned action (Azjen and

Fishbein, 1977) are predominant in the interpretation of recycling behavior. In contrast, we have found that anyone who has agreed to make a commitment to a block leader is not yet convinced but is much more likely to change his/her beliefs and attitudes with time by a desired conduct effect. This assumes that people use observations of their own behavior to determine what their ecological conscience and attitude toward recycling are, just as they assume that they know the attitudes of others by watching social norms. Therefore, this result is relevant to the low-involvement hierarchy, since it involves situations in which recycling behaviors are initially adopted in the absence of a strong internal attitude. However, as the cognitive and evaluative components fall into line after recycling behavior, and considering that the classic hierarchy of effect is predominant in understanding recycling responses, the sustained conduct must be in keeping with a classic protocol of effects. From this interpretation we have found that to achieve a high commitment to recycling as a result of this particular technique effect, it takes some time for people to be able to reduce their dissonance by feeling their own committed conduct.

From a practical point of view, this research leads to recommendations that may serve to improve environmental education plans. This makes it logical to recommend that the first step in environmental recommendation would be to explain where, how, and why citizens are expected to recycle so that they increase their recycling beliefs and emphasis should be put on attitudes toward recycling and ecological conscience because these components appear to be linked to the maintenance of the desired behavior. In other words, it makes it clear that environmental education must start by concentrating more on recycling activities. This starting point must be one of practical necessity since the consistency principle follows behavior. Afterward, the recycling act takes the first step toward ecological conscience and recycling attitudes. In short, the motto could be "learning through acting."

REFERENCES

Alwitt, Linda and Robert Pitts (1996), "Predicting Purchase Intentions for an Environmentally Sensitive Product," *Journal of Consumer Psychology,* 5(1) 49-64.

Arcury, Thomas, Timothy Johnson, and Susan Scollay (1986), "Ecological Worldview and Environmental Knowledge: The New Environmental Paradigm," *Journal of Environmental Education, 17,* 35-40.

Aronson, Elliot (1999), "Dissonance, Hypocrisy, and the Self-Concept," in *Cognitive Dissonance: Progress on a Pivotal Theory in Social Psychology,* ed. E. Harmon-Jones and J. Mills, Washington, DC: American Psychological Association, 127-147.

Azjen, Icek and Martin Fishbein (1977), "Attitude Behavior Relations: A Theoretical Analysis and Review of Empirical Research," *Psychological Bulletin, 84,* 888-918.

Bagozzi, Richard and Pratibha Dabholkar (1994), "Consumer Recycling Goals and Their Effect on Decisions to Recycle: A Mean End Chain Analysis," *Psychology and Marketing, 11,* 1-28.

Bigné, Enrique (1997): "El consumidor verde: bases de un modelo de comportamiento," Esic-Market, 237-251.

Biswas, Adhijit, Jane Licata, Daryl McKee, Chris Pullig, and Christopher Daughtridge (2000), "The Recycling Cycle: An Empirical Examination of Consumer Waste Recycling and Recycling Shopping Behaviors," *Journal of Public Policy and Marketing, 19,* 93-105.

Black, Stanley, Paul Stern, and Julie Elworth (1985), "Personal and Contextual Influences on Household Energy Adaptations," *Journal of Applied Psychology, 70,* 3-21.

Bohlen, Greg; Bodo Schlegelmilch, and Adamantios Diamantopoulos (1993), "Measuring Ecological Concern: A Multi-Construct Perspective," *Journal of Marketing Management, 9,* 415-430.

Bryce, Wendy, Rachel Day, and Thomas Olney (1997), "Commitment Approach to Motivating Community Recycling: New Zealand Curbside Trial," *The Journal of Consumers Affairs, 31*(1), 27-53.

Burn, Shawn (1991), "Social Psychology and the Stimulation of Recycling Behaviors: The Block-Leader Approach," *Journal of Applied Social Psychology, 21*(8), 611-629.

Burn, Shawn and Stuart Oskamp (1986), "Increasing Community Recycling with Persuasive Communication and Public Commitment," *Journal of Applied Social Psychology, 16*(1), 29-41.

Carey, R., S. Clicque, B. Leighton, and F. Milton (1976), "A Test of Positive Reinforcement of Customers," *Journal of Marketing, 40,* 98-100.

Chan, R. and L. Lau (2000), "Antecedents of Green Purchases: A Survey in China," *Journal of Consumer Marketing, 17*(4), 338-357.

Deleon, Iser and R. Fuqua (1995), "The Effect of Public Commitment and Group Feedback on Curbside Recycling," *Environment and Behavior, 27*(2), 233-250.

Dwyer, William, Frank Leeming, Melisa Cobern, Bryan Porter, and John Jackson (1993), "Critical Review of Behavioral Interventions to Preserve the Environment: Research Since 1980," *Environment and Behavior, 25,* 275-321.

Emmet, Robert (1990), "Understanding Paper Recycling in an Institutionally Supportive Setting: An Application of the Theory of Reasoned Action," *Journal of Environmental Systems, 19*(4), 307-321.

Festinger, Leon and James Carlsmith (1959), "Cognitive Consequences of Forced Compliance," *Journal of Abnormal and Social Psychology, 58,* 203-210.

Fishbein, Martin (1963), "An Investigation of the Relationships Between Beliefs about an Object and The Attitude Toward the Object," *Human Relations, 16,* 233-240.

Folz, David (1991), "Recycling Program Design, Management and Participation: A National Survey of Municipal Experience," *Public Administration Review, 51*(3), 222-231.

Gamba, Raymon and Stuart Oskamp (1994), "Factors Influencing Community Residents Participation in Commingled Curbside Recycling Programs," *Environment and Behavior, 26*(5), 587-612.

Geller, Scott, Jeanne Chafee, and Richard Ingram (1975), "Promoting Paper Recycling on a University Campus," *Journal of Environmental Systems, 5*(1), 39-57.

Geller, Scott (1989), "Applied Behavior Analysis and Social Marketing: An Integration for Environmental Preservation," *Journal of Social Issues, 45*(1) 17-36.

Grunert, Suzanne and Hans Jorn (1995), "Values, Environmental Attitudes, and Buying of Organic Foods," *Journal of Consumer Marketing, 16*, 39-62.

Hamad, Charles, Robert Bettinger, Donald Cooper and George Semb (1980), "Using Behavioral Procedures to Establish an Elementary School Paper Recycling Program," *Journal of Environmental Systems, 10*, 149-156.

Hopper, Joseph and Joyce Nielsen (1991), "Recycling as Altruistic Behavior. Normative and Behavioral Strategies to Expand Participation in a Community Recycling Residence," *Environment and Behavior, 23*(2), 195-220.

Hornik, Jacob, Joseph Cherian, Michelle Madansky, and Chem Narayana (1995), "Determinants of Recycling Behavior: A Synthesis of Research Results," *The Journal of Socio-Economics, 24*(1), 105-127.

Hutton, Bruce and Frank Markley (1991), "The Effects of Incentives on Environment-Friendly Behaviors: A Case of Study," *Advances in Consumer Research, 18*, 697-702.

Katzev, Richard and Anton Pardini (1987), "The Comparative Effectiveness of Reward and Commitment Approaches in Motivating Community Recycling," *Journal of Environmental Systems, 17*, 93-113.

Kok, Gerjo and Sjef Siero (1985), "Tin Recycling: Awareness, Comprehension, Attitude, Intention and Behavior," *Journal of Economic Psychology, 16*, 157-173.

Leeming, Frank, William Dwyer, Bryan Porter, and Melissa Cobern (1993), "Outcome Research in Environmental Education: A Critical Review," *Journal of Environmental Education, 24*, 8-21.

Lutz, Richard (1991), "The Role of Attitude Theory in Marketing," en Kassarjian y Robertson (eds), *Perspectives in Consumer Behavior*, Prentice Hall, 317-339.

McCaul, Kevin and John Kopp (1982), "Effects of Goal Setting and Commitment on Increasing Metal," *Journal of Applied Psychology, 67*, 377-379.

McGuiness, James, Allan Jones, and Steven Cole (1977), "Attitudinal Correlates of Recycling Behavior," *Journal of Applied Psychology, 62*, 376-384.

McKenzie-Mohr, Doug (1999), "Fostering Sustainable Behavior," *New Society Publisher*.

Minton, Ann and Randall Rose (1997), "The Effects of Environmental Concern on Environmentally Friendly Consumer Behavior: An Exploratory Study," *Journal of Business Research, 40*, 37-48.

Moreno, Ramón and Jesús López (1985), "Análisis metodológico de investigaciones experimentales en psicología," Editorial Alamex, s.a. Madrid.

O´Keefe, Daniel (2002), "Persuasion: Theory and Research," London: Sage Publications.

Oskamp, Stuart, Maura Harrington, Todd Edwards, Deborah Sherwood, Shawn Okuda, and Deborah Swanson (1991), "Factors Influencing Household Recycling Behavior," *Environment and Behavior, 23*(4), 494-519.

Pardini, Andrew and Richard Katzev (1983), "The Effect of Strength of Commitment on Newspaper Recycling," *Journal of Environmental Systems, 13,* 245-254.

Peattie, Kenneth (1990), "Panting Marketing Education (Or How To Recycle Old Ideas)," *Journal of Marketing Management, 2,* 105-125.

Ratneshwar, S., David Glen, and Cynthia Huffman (2003), *"The Why of Consumption: Contemporary Perspectives on Consumer Motives, Goals and Desires,"* London: Routledge Taulor and Francis Group.

Simmons, Deborah and Ron Widmar (1990), "Motivations and Barriers to Recycling: Toward a Strategy for Public Education," *Journal of Environmental Education, 12,* 13-18.

Shrum, L., John McCarthy, and Tina Lowrey (1995), "Understanding the Buyer Characteristics of the Green Consumer: Implications for Advertising Strategy," *Journal of Advertising, 24,* 71-82.

Spaccarelli, Steve, Edwin Zolik, and Leonard Jason (1989), "Effect of Verbal Prompting and Block Characteristics on Participation in Curbside Newspaper Recycling," *Journal of Environmental Systems, 19,* 45-57.

Steel, Carl (1988), "The Psychology of Self-Affirmation: Sustaining the Integrity of the Self," in *Advances in Experimental Social Psychology,* ed. L. Berkowitz, San Diego, CA: Academic Press, 21, 261-302.

Swanson, David (1991), "Factors Influencing Household Recycling Behavior," *Environment and Behavior, 23*(4), 494-519.

Vining, Joanne and Angela Ebreo (1989), "An Evaluation of the Public Response to a Community Recycling Education Program," *Society and Natural Resource, 2,* 23-36.

Vining, Joanne and Angela Ebreo (1990), "Whats Makes A Recycler? A Comparison Of Recyclers and Non-Recyclers, *Environmental and Behavior, 22*(1), 55-73.

Wang, Teodore and Richard Katzev (1990), "Group Commitment and Resource Conservation: Two Field Experiments on Promoting Recycling," *Journal of Applied Social Psychology, 20,* 265-275.

Wesley, Paul, Stuart Oskamp, and Tina Mainieri (1995), "Who Recycles and When? A Review Of Personal And Situational Factors," *Journal of Environmental Psychology, 15,* 105-121.

Williams, E. (1991), "College Students and Recycling: Their Attitudes and Behaviors," *Journal of College Student Development, 32,* 86-88.

Zimmer, Mary; Thomas Stafford, and Marla Royne, (1994), "Green Issues: Dimensions of Environmental Concern," *Journal of Business Research, 30,* 63-74.

doi:10.1300/J054v17n01_04

The Internet in Social Marketing Research

Julian de Meyrick

SUMMARY. Social marketing campaigns are usually aimed at problems that exact a large toll in the community. Any campaign must be properly researched during the development process and afterward, to assess its impact. The target market for social marketing campaigns often includes younger members of the community. The research methodology used when developing or assessing these campaigns must therefore be appropriate to adolescents.

This article discusses the application of Internet technology to research among adolescents using experience gained while testing potential anti-smoking messages among a sample of UK school students to illustrate the issues.

Internet-based research has the potential to generate data that is comparable to that generated by conventional research methods and with improved efficiency in terms of timescale, cost, quality, and quantity of responses. doi:10.1300/ J054v17n01_05 *[Article copies available for a fee from The Haworth Document Delivery Service: 1-800-HAWORTH. E-mail address:*

Julian de Meyrick is a lecturer in Marketing in the Business Department, Macquarie University, NSW 2109, Australia. His principal research interest is social marketing, especially anti-smoking marketing (E-mail: julian.demeyrick@mq.edu.au).

The author would also like to acknowledge the invaluable help of the anonymous reviewer and Dr. Peter Petocz, my guide through SPSS. The UK study discussed in this article would not have been possible without the support and guidance provided by the Health Education Unit while Julian was a Visiting Fellow at the University of Southampton, UK.

[Haworth co-indexing entry note]: "The Internet in Social Marketing Research." de Meyrick, Julian. Co-published simultaneously in *Journal of Nonprofit & Public Sector Marketing* (Best Business Books, an imprint of The Haworth Press, Inc.) Vol. 17, No. 1/2, 2007, pp. 103-120; and: *Social Marketing: Advances in Research and Theory* (eds: Debra Z. Basil and Walter Wymer) Best Business Books, an imprint of The Haworth Press, Inc., 2007, pp. 103-120. Single or multiple copies of this article are available for a fee from The Haworth Document Delivery Service [1-800-HAWORTH, 9:00 a.m. - 5:00 p.m. (EST). E-mail address: docdelivery@haworthpress.com].

KEYWORDS. Social marketing, Internet, adolescents, smoking

BACKGROUND

Social marketing campaigns are usually aimed at problems that exact a large toll in the community. It is essential, therefore, that recommendations for social marketing campaigns aimed at addressing these problems have a strong research foundation to help improve their effectiveness. An essential element in this strong foundation is the use of appropriate research methodologies.

An example of an important social marketing issue is the damage done to the community by tobacco smoking. Tobacco smoking is the single most important cause of avoidable mortality and morbidity in the United States–this was the conclusion of the U.S. Surgeon General in 1964 and has remained the most important cause since then (U.S. Department of Health and Human Services, 1989). The World Health Organization has just upgraded their estimate of the annual death toll directly attributable to tobacco smoking to four million people per annum worldwide (Warren, Riley et al., 2000). Most of these deaths will occur in midlife and rob the victim of an average of 22 years of life (Peto, Lopez et al., 1994).

Interest in this topic remains high. A search through ABI, Proquest, and Science Direct using the words "tobacco," "morbidity," and "mortality" generated 350 full-text, refereed articles in English, including the articles mentioned above, dealing with aspects of this topic. The reported research covered developed and developing countries, ranging alphabetically from Argentina to the Ukraine, and revealed significant smoking-prevalence levels and consequent loss of quantity and quality of life in all the countries studied. English, Holman, et al., 1995) estimated that smoking killed 18,920 Australians in 1992 and caused 88,266 person years of life to be lost before age 70 years. They compared this to the estimate developed by Peto et al. (1994) of 13,984 deaths among males in Australia, or 22% of all deaths, and 4,959 deaths among females, 9% of all deaths. Later, Collins and Lapsley (1996) generated an increased estimate of 23,000 tobacco-caused deaths and a cost to the community of AU$18 billion per year. Mannino, Ford, et al. (2001) developed similar estimates for the United States.

The target market for social marketing campaigns often includes younger members of the community, so the research methodology employed must be appropriate for younger people. For example, the mean age at which young people take up smoking in most developed countries is 15. It is slightly lower in some countries and is slowly but steadily edging lower. Conversely, young people "grow out" of the need to take up smoking. If a young person has not taken up smoking by the age of 20, they are extremely unlikely to do so thereafter. This phenomenon has been identified in many countries. Although some researchers have indicated that there might be inconsistencies in the accuracy with which smokers report the age at which they took up smoking–Engels, Knibbe et al. (1997) and Kovar (2000) raise questions about the accuracy of estimates of smoking prevalence among adolescents–there is a clear pattern of early or adolescent onset of smoking (Joffe, 2001; Najem, Batuman, et al., 1997; Warren et al., 2000). The U.S. Department of Health and Human Services (1989) suggested categorizing tobacco smoking as a pediatric disease. Everett, Warren, et al. (1999) showed that there is a clear correlation between earlier smoking initiation and greater prevalence and heavier smoking later in life. This emphasizes the need to develop effective prevention campaigns aimed at adolescents.

Unfortunately, of those who do take it up before then, approximately half will become addicted and continue to smoke for the rest of their lives (Cinciripini, Hecht, et al., 1997; Pierce and Gilpin, 1996; Russell, 1990). Once addicted, a smoker finds it very difficult to quit. Cinciripini et al. (1997) and Russell (1990) report that fewer than 15% of Americans who quit smoking for one day remain abstinent one year later. This further reinforces the need for effective campaigns to reduce the onset of tobacco smoking among adolescents.

The reasons why young people take up smoking continue to be widely researched. Conrad, Flay et al. (1992), Harrell, Bangdiwala, et al. (1998) and Pomerleau, Pomerleau, et al. (1998) all examine smoking initiation, identifying factors such as peer pressure, adult role-modeling, and curiosity as common causes of smoking initiation. Other factors that have been identified include the presence of smokers in peer groups, family, and friends; the stress of passing through the changes associated with adolescence; and the need to express one's independence and to make one's own decisions in adolescence. McNeill (1991) looks at the process by which a young person takes up smoking and quickly acquires a nicotine addiction. Again, curiosity and peer pressure are reported as causal factors.

A general, sustained reduction in tobacco smoking remains an urgent social marketing priority. To reduce tobacco smoking prevalence and the consequent damage to the community, action needs to be taken both to encourage current smokers to give up (cessation) and to help young people avoid taking it up (prevention). It is unlikely that one social marketing campaign initiative will be equally effective at both tasks as they are targeted at different people and have different problems to overcome. Any campaign must be properly researched during the development process and afterward, to assess its impact.

As noted above, prevention campaigns must be targeted at adolescents if they are to reach them in time to help them avoid taking up smoking. The research methodology must therefore be appropriate to adolescents.

Literature on the use of students as subjects in research and the use of nonprobability (e.g., convenience) sampling methodologies focuses on the extent to which research results can be generalized to other populations or the population in general.

The first issue is one of generalization. Cunningham, Anderson, and Murphy (1974, 399) suggest that the "convenience and minimal cost associated with student samples make them a highly attractive data source." Courtright (1996) suggests that, because the use of these students has been so pervasive, "we are quite knowledgeable about 20-year-old college students, but hardly anyone else" (418).

In the cases discussed in most reports, the students are being called upon to represent populations that are often more heterogeneous and different in other ways from the student group. For example, James and Sonner (2001) and Peterson (2001) discuss generalizing from students to consumers in general. Cunningham et al. (1974) compare responses to a questionnaire that was administered to a class of junior-level introductory-marketing students to those received when the questionnaire was mailed to a random sample selected from the Austin, Texas, telephone directory. Robinson, Heufner, and Hunt (2001) compare responses from college-student and nonstudent entrepreneurs.

It is not surprising that the student responses often differ from those gathered from these different groups. Cunningham et al. (1974) conclude, "Thus it appears that students are not good surrogates for assessing household consumers' sociopsychological attitudes" (403).

Lynch (1982) addresses the issue of generalizing from non-probability samples and suggests that, in consumer research (rather than scientific or theoretical research) "random sampling is of less-than-crucial importance, undesirable, or utterly impossible" (226). The "less-than-crucial importance" flows from Calder, Phillips, and Tybout (1981) who suggest that "convenience samples of relatively *homogeneous* (sic) subjects are desirable" because this will increase the chance of detecting violations of the theory being tested (Lynch, 1982, 226). Some of the impossibility issues relate to the impossibility of enumerating the population and choosing respondents at random, and the problem of prematurely specifying the population when it is not clear. Lynch cites Cook and Campbell (1979) who point out, "...we are *often unsure about what the population is to which we think our results should generalize.*" But this should not prohibit the use of convenience sampling (Lynch, 1982, 226).

Mook (1983) focuses on the question of generalizability and contends that all social science experiments, including those conducted in the real world, will have limits to their generalizability because "cultural, historical, and age-group limits will surely be present; but these are unknown and no single study can discover them all" (379-80).

According to Mook, the important question should be, "Are the sample, the setting, and the manipulation so artificial that the class of target real-life situations to which the results can be generalized is likely to be trivially small?" (380)

The population of interest in this article is composed of young people in their middle-teen years. In the UK and many other similarly developed countries, most of these people are at school. It has also been shown that they have widespread access to the Internet. The issue of interest is the impact on responses of administering a survey among young people via either electronic or the conventional paper form. The settings are different for the two samples and this might introduce biases of the type that Kruglanski (1975) refers to as "artifacts." Comparison of the two sets of responses suggests that none of these biases was, in fact, present.

For these reasons, it is suggested that this methodology is appropriate to compare the results when a group of young people are surveyed using the Internet or using the conventional hard-copy methodology.

THE INTERNET

Skinner, Biscope et al. (2003) compiled the information in Table 1 showing estimates of Internet access in a selection of countries. Outside of India and China, Internet access is available to a significant proportion of the population.

Among adolescents and young people, growth in Internet access has been particularly rapid and extensive. In all countries except England

TABLE 1. Estimates of Global Internet Access, 2000-2001

	General Population (%)	Youth (%)
World	8	49
Canada	53	99
United States	42	65
England	76	75
France	20	41
Sweden	61	47
Turkey	16	22
Israel	30	56
India	9	38
Australia	50	82
China	7	13
Taiwan	31	63

Reprinted from Social Science & Medicine, Volume 57(5), Skinner, H., Biscope, S. and Po-land, B., "Quality of Internet Access: Barrier Behind Internet Use Statistics," pp. 875-880, 2003. Used with permission from Elsevier.

and Sweden, access among younger people is significantly greater than among the population in general. Delivery of a survey to young people via the Internet might have some important advantages over the traditional pencil-and-paper approach.

It is possible that the quantity and quality of responses might increase when a survey among young people and adolescents is administered via the Internet instead of via the conventional paper-and-pencil approach. To adolescents the Internet is familiar, modern technology, unlike pencil-and-paper that may be seen as dated and associated with a previous generation. Many young people are familiar with the medium and they use it regularly. Responses are seen to be entered directly into the system and may not be regarded as having been handled by an (adult) intermediary who might violate the respondent's confidentiality. The adolescents may feel more in control of the situation and this might encourage them to participate in such a survey and to be more candid in their responses.

Mounting a survey via the Internet also saves the cost of printing, postage, and recovery of the questionnaire. It can also remove the need for response coding with consequent cost savings and, possibly, improvement in data entry as Internet-based surveys offer the potential to be received directly into analytical programs such as SPSS. Finally, mounting the survey on the Internet saves time. The questionnaire can be made available to the farthest-flung target audience, completed and returned, literally in a matter of minutes rather than weeks. The data entry and analysis processes can be almost instantaneous.

Literature on traditional survey methodologies is widespread and voluminous. Interest in the impact of the spread of the Internet for researchers is gathering momentum, just as the spread of the Internet into many target markets is gathering momentum. A search of Science Direct and ABI/Proquest electronic databases for the years 1998 to 2002 inclusive yielded 15 articles of relevance to this project, with numbers increasing in each successive year.

Eight of the articles (Couper, 2001; Epstein, Klinkenberg et al., 2001; Lazar and Preece, 1999; Mertler, 2002; Monolescu and Schifter, 2000; Ting, Gross et al., 2002; Witte, Amoroso et al. 2000) relate to methodological issues such as ensuring sample equivalence or are general papers on the design of electronic surveys. The paper by Cook, Heath et al. (2001) reports on a comparison study, but of two different Internet methods for recording responses ("sliders" versus "radio buttons"), not a comparison of Internet-based methods with traditional data-gathering methods.

The remaining seven articles deal specifically with comparisons of electronic (specifically Internet-based) survey methods with traditional methods to test whether they do deliver the potential benefits. The results are equivocal and there are aspects of many of the studies that make them of questionable relevance to this project.

There were no samples in any of these studies that are directly comparable to the adolescents at the center of this study. For example, Boyer, Olson et al. (2002) used a sample of purchasers of office supplies who used the Internet to make their purchases. The Klassen and Jacobs (2001) study also used business people in the manufacturing industry; Raziano, Jayadevappa et al. (2001) surveyed chiefs of geriatric units, Harewood, Yacavone et al. (2001) followed up patients after outpatient endoscopy treatment; and Cobanoglu, Warde et al. (2001) surveyed a sample of 300 hospitality professors. It is quite possible that the relationship these groups have with the Internet is quite different from that which adolescents enjoy. For example, penetration of the Internet among adolescents is much higher than it is among many older groups and the younger group is more familiar with the technology. This might influence their reactions to an Internet-based questionnaire.

Hancock and Flowers (2001) studied the differences in Social Desirability Response (SDR) among university students completing anonymous and non-anonymous, and Internet and traditional surveys. They found no significant difference across the four options, but this might, to some extent, have been influenced by the fact that the anonymity of students completing the electronic surveys was compromised as they sat with their backs to spectators and passersby who had a clear view of the students' responses on the monitors they were using.

Knapp and Kirk (2002) also studied differences in responses to a survey among university undergraduates administered by Internet, touch-tone telephone, and traditional means. It is relevant to this project, although university undergraduates may differ in important respects from adolescents. Knapp and Kirk suggest that the extent to which the respondents are forthcoming in response to questions on sensitive topics is governed by two factors: the extent to which the respondents believe that their confidentiality is assured and their familiarity with the methodology. They feel that the lack of any significant differences among the responses via the three different methodologies is due to the fact that on these two criteria, the two methods, as presented in their experiment, are indistinguishable for the respondents.

There is the opportunity and the need to test whether the use of the Internet to administer a questionnaire to adolescent respondents will deliver a better response rate, fewer incomplete responses, and data that is otherwise comparable with data gathered using the traditional paper-and-pencil approach.

METHODOLOGY

Secondary schools were approached to allow groups of their Year 10 students (approximately 15-years-old) to participate in this project. Five secondary schools agreed to participate. One of the schools is a private girls' school located near Birmingham, England. The remaining schools are located in close proximity to the University of Southampton, England, and include a mixture of single sex, coeducational, independent and state schools. In each of the participating schools, two groups of approximately 50 students each were recruited to participate in the survey.

A short, anonymous, non-intrusive questionnaire was developed for this study. The same questionnaire was available in conventional paper form and electronic form for completion via the Internet.

A Delphi-style, anonymous, iterative consultation by e-mail with a panel of experts developed a list of 14 potential advertising messages that might help an adolescent avoid taking up cigarette smoking. The experts were drawn from advertising agencies with expertise in addressing adolescents, research organizations with expertise in researching among adolescents, and policy makers with expertise in developing, implementing, and evaluating anti-smoking campaigns. These experts were located in Australia, New Zealand, and the United Kingdom.

The 14 messages were incorporated into the questionnaire. (See Table 8 for a list of the messages.) After a filter question to separate respondents who regard themselves as either Current, Lapsed or Never smokers, respondents evaluated the messages on the extent to which they felt the message might be effective in helping an adolescent avoid taking up smoking. Evaluation was in the form of a five-point scale, 1 = not effective at all, to 5 = very effective.

Supplies of preprinted paper questionnaires were delivered to the participating teacher at each of the five participating schools. Completed questionnaires were collected and returned in a single batch from each respondent school. The URL (Internet address) where the Internet version of the questionnaire was located was also sent to the participating teachers to pass on to the sample of students who were to complete the survey electronically. These responses were returned automatically and anonymously to the researcher's e-mail address.

RESULTS

In total, 347 usable responses were received. Of these, 258 were hard-copy (paper) responses. The balance was received via the Internet. The pattern of responses from the sample schools is shown in Table 2.

In each school, the number of students given the printed questionnaire and the Internet URL was approximately equal.

Paper responses were collected from the students and returned in one batch per school. It was possible therefore, to correctly identify the respondent school in each case. Responses via the Internet included a

TABLE 2. Responses by Media and Sample School

		School						
		School 1	School 2	School 3	School 4	School 5	Missing	Total
Media	Paper	52	48	63	46	49	0	258
	Internet	24	6	33	0	17	8	89
Total		76	54	96	46	66	8	347

field in which the respondent identified their school. In eight cases, this field was empty. Comparing these responses with others received at about the same time enabled six of them to be allocated to their respondent schools.

Seven students (2.7%) who completed the paper questionnaire failed to complete four of the classification questions (age, gender, ethnicity, the presence of other, regular smokers in the family). Two of the Internet-based respondents (2.9%) omitted answers to the questions relating to gender, ethnicity, and the presence of other smokers in the respondent's home. One of these respondents also did not answer the age question.

FIGURE 1. Smoking Status (%)

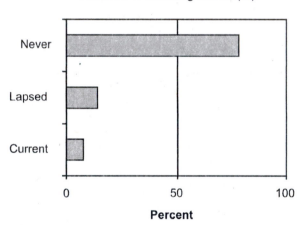

Only 26 (7.5%) of the respondents reported that they are currently regular smokers. A further 49 (14.1%) reported that they had been regular smokers in the past but had successfully given up the habit. For the purposes of analysis, these two groups were combined into a Current and Lapsed Smokers group for comparisons with the respondents who described themselves as Never having been regular smokers. The combined percentage (21.6) is comparable with levels of lifetime use of cigarettes among 15-16 year olds in the UK in 1999 by Hibbell, Andersson et al. (2000).

In relation to smoking status, there was no significant difference at the .05 level, between students who completed the paper- or Internet-based questionnaires.

TABLE 3. Smoking Status, Response Medium, Gender and Smoker in Home

		Smoking status	
		Lapsed	Never
Response medium	Paper	20.6	79.4
	Internet	23.6	76.4
Gender	Female	23.9	76.1
	Male	17.3	82.7
Smoker in home	No	10.4	89.6
	Yes	32.5	67.5

A smaller proportion of male respondents (17.3%) than female respondents (23.9%) described themselves as Lapsed or Current smokers. This is in line with current trends in smoking prevalence levels, although the difference is not significant at the .05 level.

There was a significant difference between respondents with another smoker in their home and those without, in terms of their reported smoking status. This also coincides with other studies showing that the presence of other smokers in the home or among friends is correlated with an increased risk of taking up smoking (Conrad et al., 1992; Derzon and Lipsey, 1999).

The most common reason Lapsed or Current smokers gave for taking up smoking was peer pressure (50% of responses), followed by curiosity (19%). This is consistent with the research cited above but the number of respondents in this category meant that further subdivision by gender or response medium generated cells too small for statistical analysis.

The most common reason Never smokers gave for not smoking was the health consequences of smoking (72% of responses). Health was also combined with other factors such as the effect of smoking on the skin, teeth, and breath of smokers. This was the case in 17% of responses, so health consequences were mentioned in a total of 89% responses from Never smokers, making it the dominant reason for not smoking.

The pattern was similar among male and female respondents and paper- and Internet-based responses.

TABLE 4. Most Important Reason Not to Smoke (%)

	Gender		Response Medium	
	Female	Male	Paper	Internet
Health consequences	73	73	70	81
Health + Other	18	16	19	10
Total Health Related	91	89	89	91

Males constituted a larger proportion of the Internet-based responses than they did of the paper-based, but not to a significant extent.

TABLE 5. Gender and Response Medium

		Gender		Total
		Female	Male	
Media	Paper	153	95	248
	Internet	49	38	87
	Total	202	133	335

The target group for this study is students aged 15 years, the mean age of smoking initiation. The sample was drawn from Year 10 students and the responses were concentrated within the range 14 or 15 years of age (72.0%). For the purposes of analysis, the one 17-year-old student was included in a renamed ≥ 16 category.

TABLE 6. Age of Respondents

		Frequency	Percent	Valid Percent
Valid	<14	71	20.5	21.1
	14	135	38.9	40.2
	15	115	33.1	34.2
	16	14	4.0	4.2
	17	1	.3	.3
	Total	336	96.8	100.0
Missing		11	3.2	
Total		347	100.0	

The standard ethnic-group descriptions from the UK Census were used for respondents to describe the ethnic group to which they regard themselves as belonging.

TABLE 7. Ethnicity of Respondents

		Frequency	Percent
Valid	White-British	278	80.1
	White-Other	12	3.5
	Mixed-Other	5	1.4
	A/AB-Indian	11	3.2
	Other	30	8.6
	Total	336	96.8
Missing		11	3.2
Total		347	100.0

The predominant response claimed to be White–British (80.1%), followed by White–Other (3.5%) and Indian (3.2%). The numbers in the groups other than White British were too small to provide any meaningful comparisons for further analysis.

A comparison of the mean ratings assigned to each of the 14 suggested anti-smoking messages by respondents using the email and the conventional methodology was completed using a MANOVA analysis in SPSS. Because of the number of tests, a correction was applied. Since the 14 tests are not truly independent, the full Bonnforonni correction (.05/14) was not applied rather, α was arbitrarily reduced from .05 to .01. There is no significant difference between the assessments of the students who completed the conventional paper survey and those who responded via the Internet at this lower level. Three of the tests (Smoking is addictive, Nobody wants to be with a smoker, and Smoking destroys our culture) showed a marginal difference (sig. = .050, .036 and .041 respectively). Each of these tests also showed approximately a quarter of a point difference in the mean Likert scale evaluations across the two response methods. None of the other tests showed any such difference. In Table 8 the messages are ranked according to their overall evaluation by all respondents. The two columns show their rankings according to paper-based and Internet-based responses. When considering the most important, effective messages (those with a mean rating in excess of 3.0) the rankings are very close to identical across the media.

TABLE 8. Mean Ratings and Rankings

Overall effectiveness ranking	Paper		Internet	
	Rating	Ranking	Rating	Ranking
Effective (mean rating > 3.0)				
Smoking causes medical problems	3.91	1	3.75	1
Smoking affects your appearance	3.78	2	3.66	2
Smoking affects your fitness	3.40	3	3.31	3
Smoking is addictive	3.20	4=	2.98	4
Smoking puts chemicals into your body	3.20	4=	2.93	5
Smokers spend their money on cigarettes	3.04	6	2.92	6
Neutral (mean rating approx 2.5)				
Smoking is destroying our culture	2.90	7	2.56	8
Smoking is a sign of nervousness	2.53	8	2.57	7
Smokers are being exploited	2.44	9	2.28	10
Smoking is not an adult privilege	2.37	10	2.39	9
Nobody wants to be with a smoker	2.24	11	2.00	13
Smokers are losers	2.18	12	2.20	11
Not effective (mean rating < 2.2)				
Smoking is not a safe alternative	2.02	13	2.10	12
Smoking is not cool	1.94	14	1.96	14

None of the messages was given an average rating of "more effective" or "very effective" in persuading a young person to avoid starting to smoke.

When assessing the potential messages, there was a significant difference (at the .05 probability level) between those who described themselves as Never having been regular smokers and the other respondents in five of the messages:

– Smoking is not a safe alternative to other drugs
– Smoking is not an adult privilege
– Smokers are losers
– Smoking is addictive
– Smokers spend money on cigarettes

Of the remaining nine messages, there was no significant difference between the groups at the .05 level. It is interesting that both smokers and Never smokers agree that the message relating to the health consequences of smoking is rated as the most effective of the list.

DISCUSSION

Response rates for the Internet-based survey fluctuated widely and were below the paper-based response rates. The paper-based rates were higher than might have been expected because the participating teachers, on their own initiative, handed out and collected the questionnaires and the students completed the questionnaires in the classroom. The Internet-based survey was completed without teacher supervision and is possibly more representative of the anonymous survey methodology. The response rates from three of the schools (schools 1, 3, and 4) were well in excess of what might have been expected from a completely self-administered survey of adolescents. This would tend to support the suggestion that Internet technology is familiar to adolescents and they are more likely to respond to an Internet-based survey than a conventional paper-based alternative–in the absence of teacher supervision.

The number of incomplete questionnaires can be significantly reduced, if not virtually eliminated, by using Internet-based software that can check for unanswered questions. This software was not available for this project.

In terms of the content of the response, the Internet-based survey generated results that were not significantly different from the conventional paper-based results in any important respect.

The focus on health and related consequences as the main reason to avoid smoking may well reflect the accumulated impact of repeated exposure to these messages in the health-education curriculum since primary school. Both survey methodologies revealed the same concentration on these factors among the respondents.

In terms of access to the target population, Internet access is already high in many communities and increasing rapidly, especially among younger and adolescent groups. The Internet will provide comparable access to adolescents and may in time provide superior access to them.

CONCLUSION

These results lend support to the suggestion that the Internet presents a viable alternative to the traditional, paper-based survey methodology when researching social marketing issues, especially among adolescents. In some respects, this comparison was biased against the Internet because it did not employ some of the latest technology that will greatly improve the quality of responses generated via the Internet.

Even with these disadvantages and the lower response rate, the Internet generated comparable data at a reduced cost. There is no need to print, dispatch, and retrieve paper copies of the questionnaire, and if the latest technology is employed, data entry happens automatically. The author recommends that if teacher supervision is not available and desirable, the Internet should be considered as the survey methodology when addressing social marketing issues among adolescents. Alternatively, response rates for electronically administered surveys among school students could be significantly improved (at virtually no significant extra cost) if the participation of the schoolteachers can be incorporated into the survey process.

REFERENCES

Berkowitz, L. (ed.) (1975), *Advances in Experimental Social Psychology*, New York: Academic Press, 8, 101-147.

Boyer, K. K., J. R. Olson, et al. (2002), "Print Versus Electronic Surveys: A Comparison of Two Data Collection Methodologies," *Journal of Operations Management, 20*(4), 357-373.

Calder, B. J., L. W. Phillips, and A. M. Tybout (1981), "Designing Research for Application," *Journal of Consumer Research, 8,* 197-207 cited in Lynch (2001).

Cinciripini, P. M., S. S. Hecht, et al. (1997), "Tobacco Addiction: Implications for Treatment and Cancer Prevention," *Journal of the National Cancer Institute, 89*(24), 1852-1867.

Cobanoglu, C., B. Warde, et al. (2001), "A Comparison of Mail, Fax and Web-Based Survey Methods," *International Journal of Marketing Research, 43*(4), 441-454.

Collins, D. J. and H. M. Lapsley (1996), *The Social Costs of Drug Abuse in Australia in 1988 and 1992,* Australian Government Publishing Service.

Conrad, K. M., B. R. Flay, et al. (1992), "Why Children Start Smoking Cigarettes: Predictors of Onset," *British Journal of Addiction, 87,* 1711-1724.

Cook, T. K. and D. T. Campbell (1979), *Quasi-Experimentation: Design and Analysis Issues for Field Settings,* Chicago: Rand McNally cited in Lynch (2001).

Cook, C., F. Heath, et al. (2001), "Score Reliability in Web- or Internet-Based Surveys: Unnumbered Graphic Rating Scales Versus Likert-Type Scales," *Educational and Psychological Measurement, 61*(4), 697-706.

Couper, M. P. (2001), "Web Survey Design and Administration," *Public Opinion Quarterly, 65*(2), 230-253.

Courtright, J. A. (1996), "Rationally Thinking About Nonprobability," *Journal of Broadcasting and Electronic Media, 40,* 414-421.

Cunningham, W. H., W. T. Anderson, and J. H. Murphy (1974), "Are Students Real People?" *Journal of Business, 47,* 399-409.

Derzon, J. H. and M. W. Lipsey (1999), "Predicting Tobacco Use to Age 18: A Synthesis of Longitudinal Research," *Addiction, 94*(7), 995-1006.

Engels, R. C. M. E., R. A. Knibbe, et al. (1997), "Inconsistencies in Adolescents' Self-Reports of Initiation of Alcohol and Tobacco Use," *Addictive Behaviors, 22*(5), 613-623.

English, D., C. D. A. J. Holman, et al. (1995), *The Quantification of Drug Caused Morbidity and Mortality in Australia*, Canberra, Australian Government Publishing Service.

Epstein, J., W. D. Klinkenberg, et al. (2001), "Insuring Sample Equivalence Across Internet and Paper-and-Pencil Assessments," *Computers in Human Behavior, 17*(3), 339-346.

Everett, S. A., C. W. Warren, et al. (1999), "Initiation of Cigarette Smoking and Subsequent Smoking Behavior among U.S. High School Students," *Preventive Medicine, 29*, 327-333.

Hancock, D. R. and C. P. Flowers (2001), "Comparing Social Desirability Responding on World Wide Web and Paper-Administered Surveys," *Educational Technology, Research and Development, 49*(1), 5-13.

Harewood, G. C., R. F. Yacavone, et al. (2001), "Prospective Comparison of Endoscopy Patient Satisfaction Surveys: E-Mail Versus Standard Mail Versus Telephone," *American Journal of Gastroenterology, 96*(12), 3312-3317.

Harrell, J. S., S. I. Bangdiwala, et al. (1998), "Smoking Initiation in Youth: The Roles of Gender, Race, Socioeconomics, and Developmental Status," *Journal of Adolescent Health, 23*(5), 271-279.

Hibbell, B., B. Andersson, et al. (2000), The 1999 ESPAD Report, Stockholm, The Swedish Council for Information on Alcohol and Other Drugs.

James, W. L. and B. S. Sonner (2001), "Just Say No to Traditional Student Samples," *Journal of Advertising Research,* September-October, 63-71.

Joffe, A. (2001), "Tobacco's Toll: Implications for the Pediatrician," *Pediatrics, 104*(4), 794-798.

Klassen, R. D. and J. Jacobs (2001), "Experimental Comparison of Web, Electronic and Mail Survey Technologies in Operations Management," *Journal of Operations Management, 19*(6), 713-728.

Knapp, H. and S. Kirk (2002), "Using Pencil and Paper, Internet and Touch-Tone Phones for Self-Administered Surveys: Does Methodology Matter?" *Computers in Human Behavior, 18*, 491-508.

Kovar, M. G. (2000), "Four Million Adolescents Smoke: Or Do They?" *Chance, 13*(2).

Kruglanski, A. W. (1975), "The Human Subject in the Psychology Experiment: Fact and Artifact," in Berkowitz (1975).

Lazar, J. and J. Preece (1999), "Designing and Implementing Web-Based Surveys," *The Journal of Computer Information Systems, 39*(4), 63-67.

Lynch, J. G. (1982), "On the External Validity of Experiments in Consumer Research," *Journal of Consumer Research, 9*, 225-239.

Mannino, D. M., E. Ford, et al. (2001), "Lung Cancer Mortality Rates in Birth Cohorts in the United States from 1960 to 1994," *Lung Cancer, 31*, 91-99.

McNeill, A. D. (1991), "The Development of Dependence on Smoking in Children," *British Journal of Addiction, 86*(5), 589-592.

Mertler, C. (2002), "Demonstrating the Potential for Web-Based Survey Methodology with a Case Study," *American Secondary Education, 30*(2), 49-61.

Monolescu, D. and C. Schifter (2000), "Online Focus Group: A Tool to Evaluate On-line Students' Course Experience," *The Internet and Higher Education, 2*(2-3), 171-176.

Mook, D. G. (1983), "In Defense of External Invalidity," *American Psychologist, 38,* 379-387.

Najem, G. R., F. Batuman, et al. (1997), "Patterns of Smoking Among Inner-City Teenagers: Smoking Has a Pediatric Age of Onset," *Journal of Adolescent Health, 20*(3), 226-231.

Peterson, R. A. (2001), "On the Use of College Students in Social Science Research: Insights from a Second-Order Meta-Analysis," *Journal of Consumer Research, 28,* 450-461.

Peto, R., A. D. Lopez, et al. (1994), *Mortality from Smoking in Developed Countries 1950-2000,* Oxford: Oxford University Press.

Pierce, J. P. and E. A. Gilpin (1996), "How Long Will Today's New Adolescent Smoker Be Addicted to Cigarettes?" *American Journal of Public Health, 86*(2), 253-256.

Pomerleau, O. F., C. S. Pomerleau, et al. (1998), "Early Experiences with Tobacco among Women Smokers, Ex-smokers, and Never-smokers," *Addiction, 93*(4), 595-599.

Raziano, D. B., R. Jayadevappa, et al. (2001), "E-Mail Versus Conventional Postal Mail Survey of Geriatric Chiefs," *The Gerontologist, 41*(6), 799-804.

Robinson, P. B., J. C. Huefner, and H. K. Hunt (1991), "Entrepreneurial Research on Student Subjects Does Not Generalize to Real World Entrepreneurs," *Journal of Small Business Management,* April, 42-50.

Russell, M. A. H. (1990), "The Nicotine Addiction Trap: A 40-Year Sentence for Four Cigarettes," *British Journal of Addiction, 85,* 293-300.

U.S. Dept. of Health and Human Services (1989), *Reducing the Health Consequences of Smoking: 25 Years of Progress,* A Report of the Surgeon General.

Skinner, H., S. Biscope, et al. (2003), "Quality of Internet Access: Barrier Behind Internet Use Statistics," *Social Science and Medicine, 57,* 875-880.

Ting, W., M. Gross, et al. (2002), "The Internet as a Research Tool in Complementary and Alternative Medicine: A Pilot Study," *Alternative Therapies in Health and Medicine, 8*(3), 84-86.

Warren, C. W., L. Riley, et al. (2000), "Tobacco Use by Youth: A Surveillance Report from the Global Youth Tobacco Survey Project," *Bulletin of the World Health Organisation, 78*(7), 868-876.

Witte, J. C., L. M. Amoroso, et al. (2000), "Research Methodology: Method and Representation in Internet-Based Survey Tools–Mobility, Community, and Cultural Identity," *Social Science Computer Review, 18*(2), 179-195.

doi:10.1300/J054v17n01_05

QUALITATIVE ARTICLE

Transport Behavior:
A Role for Social Marketing

Enda McGovern

SUMMARY. This article discusses travel behavior widely acknowledged to be a significant source of pollution: the use of private transport commonly referred to as the automobile. While this behavior can be tackled in a number of ways, this article presents an overview of key issues inhibiting a voluntary change in behavior among automobile users. These topics were identified based upon qualitative research data that was gathered from a number of UK households. The research methodology adopted different social marketing collateral in each of the households during the period of research. While weaknesses are identified in the marketing collateral, the research concludes that social marketing in

Enda McGovern is Associate Professor of Business at Dominican University of California and Visiting Scholar at the Institute of Transportation Studies, 50 Acacia Avenue, San Rafael, CA 94901 (E-mail: emcgovern@dominican.edu) (emcgovern@berkeley.edu).

His research interests include social marketing, travel demand and behavior, and integrated communications. Prior to joining the Faculty at Dominican, Dr. McGovern was tenured faculty at the School of Management in Brunel University, London.

[Haworth co-indexing entry note]: "Transport Behavior: A Role for Social Marketing." McGovern, Enda. Co-published simultaneously in *Journal of Nonprofit & Public Sector Marketing* (Best Business Books, an imprint of The Haworth Press, Inc.) Vol. 17, No. 1/2, 2007, pp. 121-134; and: *Social Marketing: Advances in Research and Theory* (eds: Debra Z. Basil and Walter Wymer) Best Business Books, an imprint of The Haworth Press, Inc., 2007, pp. 121-134. Single or multiple copies of this article are available for a fee from The Haworth Document Delivery Service [1-800-HAWORTH, 9:00 a.m. - 5:00 p.m. (EST). E-mail address: docdelivery@haworthpress.com].

Available online at http://jnpsm.haworthpress.com
doi:10.1300/J054v17n01_06

itself cannot persuade people to make significant changes in their travel behavior. There are deeper issues at work for commuters that need to be more fully understood by the transport research community. The value of social marketing instead may lie as an effective channel of communication that can be utilized by designated authorities in delivering important transport messages to commuters and private transport users at large. doi:10.1300/J054v17n01_06 *[Article copies available for a fee from The Haworth Document Delivery Service: 1-800-HAWORTH. E-mail address: <docdelivery@haworthpress.com> Website: <http://www.HaworthPress. com> © 2007 by The Haworth Press, Inc. All rights reserved.]*

KEYWORDS. Social marketing, transport demand management, public policy

INTRODUCTION

It is estimated that between 1950 and 1990 the number of vehicles in use worldwide grew from approximately 75 million to around 675 million (Organization for Economic Co-operation and Development, 1997). While this period coincides with an improvement in economic conditions enjoyed by industrialized countries, it could be speculated that the growth in car ownership figures was primarily linked to advances in prosperity, independence, and security. However, this shift in modal choice has created numerous problems for the environment. "Motor vehicle use is now generally recognized as the source of more air pollution than any other single human activity" (Wiederkehr, 1995, 4).

In the first few years of the twenty-first century there is little evidence to suggest that this phenomenon is about to decline. On the contrary, all indicators point to a protracted upswing in the utilization of private transport over the coming decades with few ideas forthcoming on how this may be contained. For instance, to cater to this ongoing demand, the length of the motorway network in the 15 countries of the European Union (EU15) grew by more than 25% between 1990 and 1999 to total nearly 50,000 km in 1999. As for the length of the rail network, an alternative sustainable mode of transport, it contracted by 4% in the 1990s and by 1999 was just under 154,000 km.

It is also important to observe that the use of the automobile is not just viewed as an indicator of mobility and prosperity in the industrialized countries. In underdeveloped countries where car numbers are still relatively low, such as China, India, and Pakistan, it is estimated that the number of cars worldwide would triple if they were to attain the vehicle density of the United Kingdom. The European Statistics for 2000 record the UK as having 419 passenger cars per thousand citizens while the EU15 average for the same year is recorded at 469 cars per thousand citizens (Energy and Transportation DG, 2002). A corresponding increase in the consumption of fuel and the emission of pollutants would also occur as a result of such a dramatic upsurge in traffic volume worldwide (Hunecke and Sibum, 1997).

A ROLE FOR SOCIAL MARKETING

"Altering consumption patterns is one of the greatest challenges in the quest of environmentally sound and sustainable development, given the depth to which they are rooted in the basic values and lifestyles of industrial societies throughout much of the rest of the world" (United Nations, 1992, 2). One consequence of the continued growth in the utilization of private transport is that individual access to motorized forms of transport has emerged as an important icon of progress in modern democratic societies. Consequently the freedom of movement associated with access to this personal form of mobility is hard to suppress without fear of a backlash from users. "Individual mobility is a cherished feature of the lifestyle in the economically affluent societies, satisfied by the ownership of one or more automobiles" (Bauer, 1996, 686).

As a result, national governments have been somewhat slow to challenge this behavior and have sought to stay clear of any obvious assault (e.g., punitive restrictions on use) on those people who adopt private transport. The introduction of congestion charging, launched in central London on February 17, 2003, was viewed by many as a courageous decision by the designated public authority (Transportation for London, 2003). A £5 ($8) charge is required to be paid for all vehicles travelling within the charging zone between 7:00 a.m. and 6:30 p.m., unless the vehicle is exempted.

Up until recently governments had instead diverted attention to the search for a technical solution as a means of reducing the negative environmental impacts of transport. The development of early warning communications systems on motorways that alert drivers to impending traffic congestion ahead is one example of this. The more recent development of the hybrid or electric vehicle (also referred to as *zero emissions vehicle*, or ZEV) technology is still a number of years away from becoming widely accepted by today's car owners. This is primarily due to two reasons. Firstly, the production capacity and infrastructure required to service these new vehicles will take a number of years to realize. Secondly, the operation of these alternative-powered vehicles requires a change in existing behavior to better understand limitations that may apply, for example, electric vehicles have a limited range of travel before needing to be recharged.

Nevertheless, policy makers now seem to accept that technical solutions on their own will not be sufficient to stem the anticipated scale of environmental damage. This is primarily because of an ever-increasing volume of traffic being recorded year after year. The more recent developments in out-of-town shopping centers is one example of inducing a change in travel behavior, as it creates the necessity to use the car in order to undertake the simplest of daily tasks, such as grocery shopping. Therefore, aside from governments applying the use of regulatory or fiscal instruments, what else can be done to try to stem this demand in the growth of the car as the primary mode of travel?

Any attempt to modify people's behavior lies at the heart of social marketing theory. In its formative years social marketing was primarily associated with problems directly related to health. While much of this focus continues today, there have been continuing attempts to broaden its applications into other areas such as the planting of more trees or getting householders to recycle more rubbish (Andreasen, 1995).

As social marketing theory and applications have evolved over time a more sophisticated approach to the 4Ps is emerging. In earlier social marketing campaigns the emphasis was focused primarily on promotion, namely advertising. One of the key challenges for programs today is how effective they are in engaging each of the 4Ps in the design of a successful campaign. Understanding the P, as in *promotion*, may have been the easiest application to adopt in the past as it was a simple extension of commercial marketing tactics. However, applying the 4Ps throughout the campaign can be a more difficult, costly, and onerous task for those charged with design and execution. And the application of each of the 4Ps requires a different frame of reference than those adopted for more conventional commercial marketing campaigns. Kotler, Roberto, and Lee (2002) highlight this approach by stating, "All 4Ps are considered. A winning strategy requires integrating the 4Ps, not just relying on advertising" (11).

While this is understood, this research focused on studying promotional collateral beyond just advertising at work in the field while examining transport behavior and exploring how this behavior may be influenced.

Undertaking further research on the other 3Ps is necessary to fully engage social marketing programs in their entirety on this topic of interest.

SOCIAL CHANGE PROGRAMS

Tackling environmental problems, in the majority of cases, involves some form of social change, that is, changing the way individuals and extended groups lead their lives. Ongoing efforts are made in such change programs to transform harmful practices into ones that are productive and beneficial in attempting to improve the quality of peoples' lives. But what is meant by the term "social change" in the context of developing a communications campaign? Kotler and Roberto (1989) define such a campaign as: "A social change campaign is an organized effort conducted by one group (the change agent), which intends to persuade others (the target group) to accept, modify or abandon certain ideas, attitudes, practices, and behavior" (6).

Any attempt to engineer change in society is a value-laden activity and one in which not everyone will agree upon the ends pursued or the means employed to achieve these ends (Salmon, 1989). An issue that lies at the core of programs encouraging social change is the fundamental tension between social control at one end of the scale and an individual's freedom of choice at the other end. As Kelman (1969) describes it, "for those of us who hold the enhancement of man's freedom of choice as a fundamental value, any manipulation of the behavior of others constitutes a violation of their essential humanity" (583). In order to lighten this tension, and to enable a campaign of social change to proceed, the particular issue of concern to be highlighted needs to be clearly identified and defined. It is important also that the majority of the targeted audience can identify with the issue to such an extent that they can accept it merits an intervention of some kind.

Nonetheless evidence gathered over the past twenty years suggests that a significant number of social change campaigns actually accomplish little, if any, movement in the required behavior (Kotler and Roberto, 1989). It is also recognized that such failures can breed widespread cynicism among social reformers and citizens alike. It is only through examining past campaigns in detail that deficiencies can be documented that contributed to the failure of any particular campaign.

In the past these examinations have focused on questions of *outcome* rather than *process* (Devine and Hirt, 1989). Adopting such an approach can limit the opportunity to learn from the campaign under investigation.

While it is possible to evaluate whether a campaign was a success or failure by examining the outcomes, it is not possible to examine conclusively why the campaign was a success or otherwise. It is important therefore that campaigns should be examined in regard to the process that was adopted for each one. This would facilitate a review of how each program was created as well as review the merits of its success or failure.

The most common deficiencies identified in social marketing programs include: targeting the wrong audience; weaknesses in the message appeal; early target adopters not being offered alternative options as a way to respond constructively; campaigns being underfunded; and finally the setting of unrealistic goals and objectives. It is possible to address each of these weaknesses at the outset if the correct approach and appropriate methods are adopted for each campaign. Nevertheless, many campaigns have fallen short of their goals because the target adopters and their needs were not well researched, the medium used to communicate the information was poorly chosen, or the budgets allocated were deemed to have been inadequate to mount an effective campaign.

A SHIFT IN THE MARKETING PARADIGM

Sheth and Parvatiyar (1995) argue the necessity for a shift in the approach to marketing so as to facilitate the success of social marketing programs. They identify two components: first, shaping customer needs and expectations, and the second to providing customers with appropriate choices to meet these needs. This article primarily concerns itself with the first component, that is, emphasizing the necessity to adjust or modify the requirements of car drivers' needs or expectations.

Sheth and Parvatiyar (1995) maintain that it is critical for these two components of shaping needs and providing alternatives to occur simultaneously. The scope for consumers to alter their thinking by becoming more environmentally conscious, in terms of their needs and wants, must be supplemented by the availability of new or improved products and services. Only then will it allow consumers the opportunity to alter their actual behavior as a consequence. The choices offered should meet current needs without sacrificing the ability of society to meet its future needs, that is, adhering to the principle of sustainability: "The true socio-ecological product is one that becomes a consumer's first choice, since it meets his/her consumption needs along with his/her need for a healthy, sustainable physical environment. It is important to understand that customer needs are not, nor should they be, in conflict with environmental needs. In fact, the two needs occur concurrently. People need and want to coexist with nature" (Sheth and Parvatiyar, 1995, 7).

In the transport sector this is proving difficult to achieve due to the nature of the car industry and its near total reliance on the internal combustion engine to power its product range. The question must therefore be posed: *Is it possible to communicate effectively to private transport users that their behavior may be detrimental to the environment?* And, if successful in achieving this, is it possible for the campaign to go on and induce a voluntary change in behavior to such an extent that car-drivers might begin to contemplate using alternative modes of transport? Over the past years this shift in behavior has not materialized despite significant efforts by various organizations to make car-drivers more aware of the issues. Instead of observing a decrease in the use of the motor car over this period, there has not only been a continuous rise in its daily use but also a sequential rise in the levels of car ownership (Department of Transport, 1996).

Although alternative-powered vehicles are becoming more widely available in the United States (primarily due to legislation enforced by the state of California forcing car makers to produce and sell ZEVs), they are viewed as an innovative choice in the UK. At this time it is not possible to offer the private motorist comparable choices to the motor car that are pollution free and widely available. The alternative choices of transport on offer, such as the bus or train, will have to meet with what car-drivers, as rational consumers, may deem to be "appropriate alternative choices" to the motor car. This, in turn, implies that a greater reliance needs to be placed by social marketers on shaping customers needs and wants from within existing transportation offerings. Informing private commuters of the potential risks they may encounter if they continue with their present behavior is an important part of shaping customer needs.

Research undertaken by this author (McGovern, 2000) suggests that many commuters do not comprehend that their existing transport behavior may have a detrimental effect on the quality of their lives, health related or otherwise. While there is some acknowledgement that there may be a negative effect on the health of future generations, the research participants consider this to be a problem that should be solved by those same generations. Or this could be viewed as participants simply disguising the fact that they are not willing to change their behavior regardless of the consequences for the next generation. Participants did accept, however, that they would give greater consideration to modifying their existing transport behavior if there was a stronger link established between this behavior and the specific harmful effect on mankind.

THE COMMUNICATION OF RISK

The effective communication of risk, a constituent of social marketing, is widely held to be a vital element in the success of social marketing programs and can be defined as: "The flow of information and risk evaluations back and forth between academic experts, regulatory practitioners, interest groups and the general public" (Leiss, 1996, 86).

Beck (1992) puts forward the idea that the transition from modernity to late modernity is one from an industrialized society to that of a risk society, that is, the social production of wealth is accompanied by the social production of risks. In other words the greater threat of risks is to be expected from the way modern society has taken shape. He states that, "Risk may be defined as a systematic way of dealing with hazards and insecurities induced and introduced by modernization itself" (21).

The transition for Beck from a modern to a late-modern society is also a transition from an industrial society to a risk society in which hazards are continuously being produced on a regular basis. Industrial society and risk society are, for Beck, distinct social formations: "The axial principle of the industrial society is the distortion of goods, while that of the risk society is the distribution of 'bads' or 'dangers'" (3).

The underlying proposition of Beck's theory is that because of the strength in the economic success of industrialized societies, the degree of exposure to risk is becoming more prevalent across all sections of society regardless of class–"poverty is hierarchic, smog is democratic" (36). Beck also builds a strong case that these risks differ from risks of the early part of the twentieth century because they can induce systematic and irreversible harm while they remain undetectable to the senses. However, he admits that the consequences of these risks are slowly becoming more visible to the general public, 'The latency phase of risk threats is coming to an end. The invisible hazards are becoming more visible–instead they strike home more clearly our eyes, ears and noses" (55).

TOPICS IMPEDING VOLUNTARY BEHAVIORAL CHANGE

The area known as South Bucks District, located in the southern half of Buckinghamshire County approximately 20 miles west of central London, was selected as the research site. The empirical research and analysis were undertaken between 1998 and 2000 and were divided into two phases encompassing a combination of focus-group discussions and a diary panel survey. Over a period of 10 months the participants evaluated their travel behavior in light of reviewing social marketing messages. The research program facilitated the design of research instruments that could gather and analyze data related to these travel experiences at specific times over an extended period that suited each of the participants. The key issues that undermined the participant's ability to act positively in response to the social marketing messages are now briefly reviewed.

POOR PERCEPTION OF PUBLIC TRANSPORT

Adopting public transport, either the bus or train service, was identified as the only real alternative to that of the automobile for the majority of journeys undertaken during the course of the research. Essentially this was because the average distance traveled by each household was too far to either walk or cycle. Nonetheless, the consideration of public transport, and in particular the use of the bus service, received widespread comments of dissatisfaction from the respondents and these comments encompassed many different issues.

Poor reliability of the bus services was cited in the discussions by many of the respondents as the main reason for not attempting to use the service. "The service is infrequent," says one respondent. Another participant states that "people do not think about them (buses) really because they are so infrequent." A direct link is constructed by the participants between the issue of poor reliability and the low levels of usage recorded in the research site. The participants expressed frustration in having to wait any period of time for a bus to arrive.

This point is extended further by the continuous reference to the issue of poor timetabling. The timetable was identified to be of importance because the participants were interpreting it as a form of contract or as a declaration of commitment by the transport company to provide them, as passengers, with certain travel services. The respondents quickly determined, however, that the timetable was of little value as they established that the bus companies rarely adhered to it with any sense of urgency. This seeming unwillingness by the bus companies to comply with their own schedule of services implied to them, as customers, that they were not considered important. Not maintaining the timetable therefore was seen to represent an act of bad faith on behalf of the bus companies.

This issue was perceived differently by those participants who adopted private transport everyday. They were of the opinion that they effectively designed and implemented their own personal timetable every day, a significant benefit in the quality of their chosen lifestyles. This flexibility allowed them the freedom to decide when to arrive and depart any of their chosen destinations whether for work, school, or social purposes. Providing a greater frequency of buses on routes and better fulfillment with the timetable were suggested as positive steps for the bus companies in attempting to address this negative perception.

Personal Safety

It could be argued from the research findings that the issue of personal safety is one of the main reasons people are adopting private transport in greater numbers. This concern for safety was mentioned primarily in regard to other members of the participant's immediate families who occasionally use public transport, especially females and children. This was inferred to further in the discussions when reference was made to the fact that households were becoming more *insular* in the way they lead their lives. Or how a *rtificial bubble'* were being created in order to allow members of the household to feel more secure when undertaking day-to-day journeys.

However, these expressions of concern did not relate to the direct use of public transport, that is, people were not concerned when they were actually traveling on the public mode of transport itself. The comments concerned the greater potential for unpleasant incidents to occur indirectly when using public transport, for example waiting at bus stops extended periods of time or walking home from the train station. A degree of anxiety existed among the participants in being able to safely walk the streets at different times of the day. At no point did the narrative refer in any way to dangers associated when actually traveling on any mode of public transport.

While the participants acknowledged how difficult it is to feel completely safe in any mode of transport, there was general consensus that private transport provided the greatest sense of safety for those who considered it a priority and the female participants were strongest in support of this argument. Increasing police on the beat and improved lighting at bus stops were suggested as ways of creating a better sense of security. Nonetheless, the issue of personal safety carried with it a negative consequence for many of the participants contemplating public transport.

Social Class and Choice of Transport

It was agreed among the participants, somewhat reluctantly, that a connection could be made between mode of travel and the perception of an individual's standing within the local community. One participant mentioned that the train is something that the commuter will easily accept but the bus, as he puts it, "is very down market." Positioning the bus service so low down in the social domain of transport could be viewed as a serious distraction for many commuters from utilizing the bus service for everyday journeys. The lack of anonymity in the research site seemed to perpetuate this feeling, as there seemed to be no reluctance by any of the participants in taking the bus when traveling in London. Encouraging public transport modes as socially acceptable forms of transport in both urban and rural locations needs to be acknowledged and pursued by policy makers. For example, this could take the shape of more investment in the quality of the bus fleet. However, bus operators, faced with declining usage among commuters, are forced with having to cut back on the service rather than deciding on further capital outlay.

Some of the other participants, however, take another view on this. "It is not so much that it is down market it is simply that it is a very poor service," is how one participant puts it. Another participant interjects in support of this as she believes that the bus service is not used as it is simply not good enough. She objects that it has anything to do with social compliance and, upon reflection, she supports the view that if the bus service were improved there would be a corresponding increase in the number of Gerrards Cross residents making use of the service.

Noise Pollution and the Generation Gap

Traffic noise was an issue of concern by the respondents and was particularly noticeable by the way it was criticized among the older participants but yet accepted as a normal part of everyday life by the younger ones. Comments in the narrative range from "the noise is terrible now" to "I can't say that I noticed it."

Noise pollution also acted as a catalyst in opening up other areas of disagreement between the participants. These differences can be best broken down between the different age groups of those involved. However, they all seemed to focus on one reflection; different generations have different demands. The older participants were happier if the locality remained as it was some twenty years earlier and one family even considered moving out the area into the countryside as a direct result of the changes they had observed in recent times. The younger participants expressed no such concerns and were happy to witness the area moving on and keeping up with the modern pace of life, or as moving from a rural to an urban setting over time.

During the discussion on concerns for the future, it was noticeable that the older participants looked across the room at the younger participants with an inquisitive mind. They seemed to be enquiring whether the young participants were still willing to change their behavior and there was agreement by many of the older participants on this point. Their remaining commuting time was of little consequence to the long-term problems that lie ahead. One could question the other reasons for such inaction on behalf of the older generation of participants but the younger participants were quite simply having none of it. The car represented to them a strong expression of freedom and they intended to get the opportunity to enjoy using it. During the discussions many of the younger participants claimed that they needed access to a car in order to lead an enjoyable and fulfilling life. Judging from the uncertainty among the generations of what action should be taken one could surmise that the older participants are waiting for the younger ones to undertake the desired behavior changes, while the younger participants may be waiting for the scientific community to come up with solutions to these problems.

CONCLUSIONS

This article sets out a case in support of the use of social marketing applications in the field of transport studies. It attempts to build an academic argument by linking together the relevant theories in support of a grounded course of action. A number of key components are identified in trying to better understand the process of how people make transport decisions as well as getting a more thorough appreciation of the transport behavior itself. Emphasis was placed in the research on the necessity to adjust or modify the requirements of car drivers' needs or expectations. The research concludes that in order to do this successfully, and to be able to produce the appropriate social marketing appeals, the concerned public authority must gain a better understanding of the issues affecting the decision-making process of the everyday commuter.

The issues briefly reviewed in this article in support of commuters concerns are an essential part of the *process* versus *outcome* discussed earlier in this article. The needs of the commuter can only be accurately assessed if the research facilitates an extended period of consultation, that is, the extensive period of time spend communicating with the participants in this research, approximately 10 months, enabled a much deeper insight of the issues to be harvested from the data. As a result, social marketers primed with this knowledge would be better empowered to create stronger social marketing programs with a much greater potential for positive results.

IMPLICATIONS FOR SOCIAL MARKETING

Social marketing has a very important role to play in the area of transport behavior in the coming years. Notwithstanding the importance of the environment and the related financial costs associated with congestion on an annual basis, an overreliance on the automobile by society at large is having a considerable effect on the health of certain population segments.

The continued progress of social marketing theory within this domain requires that marketers come together with a broad array of experts including those in public policy making, transport engineers, sociologists, urban planners, and many more. More research needs to be undertaken on how transport behavior can be modified to more quickly embrace the latest developments such as the mainstreaming of alternative-powered vehicles, the advances in information technology facilitating a greater choice of work locations, and the pay-as-you-travel concept in road pricing. There is an urgent need for the accumulation of more in-depth research data on this most important facet of everyday life.

REFERENCES

Andreasen, A. (1995), *Marketing Social Change: Changing Behavior to Promote Health, Social Development, and the Environment*, San Francisco: Jossey-Bass Publishers.

Bauer, M. (1996), "Transport And The Environment: Can Technology Provide The Answers?" *Energy Policy, 24* (8), 685-687.

Beck, U. (1992), *Risk Society: Toward a New Modernity,* London: Sage Publications.

Department Of Transport. (DoT) (1996), "Transport: The Way Forward," *Command Paper 3234*, London: HMSO.

Devine, P. and E. Hirt (1989) "Message Strategies for Information Campaigns: A Social-Psychological Analysis," in *Information Campaigns: Balancing Social Values and Social Change,* ed. C. Salmon, London: Sage Annual Review of Communication Research, 18, 229-258.

Eurostat, (2002), *Transport Infrastructure in Europe Between 1990 And 1999,* Brussels: No 43/2002.

ENERGY and TRANSPORTATION DG. (2002), http://europa.eu.int/comm/energy_transport/etif/transport_means_road/motorization.html.

Hunecke, M. and D. Sibum (1997), *Socio-Economic Aspects of Individual Mobility,* Brussels: Report EUR 17712 EN.

Kelman, G. (1969), "Manipulation of Human Behaviors: An Ethical Dilemma for the Social Scientist," in *The Planning of Change,* ed. W. Bennis, K. Benne, and R. Chin, New York: Holt, 582-595.

Kotler, P. and E. Roberto (1989), *Social Marketing: Strategies for Changing Public Behavior,* New York: The Free Press.

Kotler, P., E. Roberto, and N. Lee, (2002), *Social Marketing: Improving the Quality of Life,* Second Ed, Thousand Oaks: Sage Publications.

Leiss, W. (1996), "Three Phases in the Evolution of Risk Communication Practice," in *Challenges in Risk Assessment and Risk Management, The Annals of the American Academy of Political and Social Science,* 545 (May 1996), 85-94.

McGovern, E. (2000), *The Role and Influence of Social Marketing in the Evolution of the Environmental Citizen,* PhD Thesis, London.

Organization for Economic Co–Operation and Development (OECD) (1997), *Sustainable Consumption and Individual Travel Behavior: Report of the OECD Policy Meeting,* Paris: OCDE/GD(97)144.

Salmon, C. (1989),"Campaigns for Social "Improvement": An Overview of Values, Rationales and Traits," in *Information Campaigns: Balancing Social Values and Social Change,* ed. C. Salmon, London: Sage Annual Review of Communication Research, 18, 19-53.

Sheth, J. and A. Parvatiyar (1995), "Ecological Imperatives and the Role of Marketing," in *Environmental Marketing: Strategies, Practice, Theories, and Research,* ed. M. Polonsky and A. Mintu-Wimsatt, New York: The Haworth Press, 3-20.

Transportation For London (2003), *Central London Congestion Charging Scheme: Three Months On,* London: Congestion Charging Division.

United Nations (1992), *The Global Partnership for Environment and Development: A Guide to Agenda 21,* Geneva: UNCED.

Wiederkehr, P. (1995), *Motor Vehicle Population: Reduction Strategies Beyond 2010,* Paris: Organization for Economic Co-operation and Development (OECD).

doi:10.1300/J054v17n01_06

CONCEPTUAL FRAMEWORK ARTICLE

A Typology of Charity Support Behaviors:
Toward a Holistic View of Helping

John Peloza
Derek N. Hassay

SUMMARY. Charities and researchers have begun to adopt a much broader view of support; one that transcends traditional forms of consumer charitable support behavior (CSB) such as donations and volunteerism to include cause-related marketing (CRM), charity events and charity gaming. The current article builds upon this expanding view of charity support by introducing a typology of CSB that encompasses the breadth of consumer CSB. In doing so, the article provides direction for charities

John Peloza is a PhD student in the Marketing Area at the Haskayne School of Business at the University of Calgary, 2500 University Avenue N.W., Calgary, Alberta, Canada, T2N 1N4 (john.peloza@haskayne.ucalgary.ca).

Derek N. Hassay is Assistant Professor in the Marketing Area at the Haskayne School of Business at the University of Calgary.

The authors contributed equally to the development of this article, and would like to thank Debra Basil and the Centre for Socially Responsible Marketing at the University of Lethbridge.

[Haworth co-indexing entry note]: "A Typology of Charity Support Behaviors: Toward a Holistic View of Helping." Peloza, John, and Derek N. Hassay. Co-published simultaneously in *Journal of Nonprofit & Public Sector Marketing* (Best Business Books, an imprint of The Haworth Press, Inc.) Vol. 17, No. 1/2, 2007, pp. 135-151; and: *Social Marketing: Advances in Research and Theory* (eds: Debra Z. Basil and Walter Wymer) Best Business Books, an imprint of The Haworth Press, Inc., 2007, pp. 135-151. Single or multiple copies of this article are available for a fee from The Haworth Document Delivery Service [1-800-HAWORTH, 9:00 a.m. - 5:00 p.m. (EST). E-mail address: docdelivery@haworthpress.com].

Available online at http://jnpsm.haworthpress.com
doi:10.1300/J054v17n01_07

seeking to garner additional support from current supporters, as well as a means of attracting new supporters by using non-traditional forms of charitable support. doi:10.1300/J054v17n01_07 *[Article copies available for a fee from The Haworth Document Delivery Service: 1-800-HAWORTH. E-mail address: <docdelivery@haworthpress.com> Website: <http://www.Haworth Press.com> © 2007 by The Haworth Press, Inc. All rights reserved.]*

KEYWORDS. Charitable support, cause marketing, charity events, charity

INTRODUCTION

Charities are facing an increasingly competitive fund-raising environment. Chronic funding shortages are the result of factors such as an ever-increasing number of charities in need of funds (Liao, Foreman, and Sargeant, 2001) and decreasing direct donations (Williamson, 2003). There is also increased competition for volunteers (Bussell and Forbes, 2002). These conditions have forced charities to become more aggressive in trying to find new ways to attract and maintain both donor and volunteer support. There has also been a concomitant increase in the variety of revenue-producing approaches employed by charitable organizations, such as charity-branded products (Bennett and Gabriel, 2000), charity lotteries/raffles (Peloza and Hassay, 2004), and cause-related marketing (Varadarajan and Menon, 1988). Akin to fund-raising, these novel approaches to revenue generation reflect new ways for the public to support charities–what the authors refer to as charity support behaviors (CSB).

The academic literature associated with CSB has almost exclusively focused on financial donations and volunteerism. Although cause-related marketing has received considerable attention of late, there is a need for an expanded view of CSB and more research on non-conventional forms of CSB. This expanded view of helping behavior is critical for charities that seek to maximize opportunities to gain support from current supporters, and provide opportunities to introduce the work of the charity to those potential supporters. To this end, the authors propose a typology that provides practitioners with an overview of all of the support opportunities available to their charity. The typology also offers charities a novel perspective on segmenting the charity support market and offers insight on how they might attract support from a previously untapped market of supporters. Finally, the proposed typology provides researchers with a framework that integrates previous research efforts and a guide to future research opportunities. For instance, the typology introduces and promotes forms of CSB that have received little attention in the non-profit literature (e.g., charity products), and provides researchers with insight into a variety of new areas of inquiry, such as consumer perceptions of novel forms of CSB.

The article begins with a discussion of the theoretical underpinnings of the CSB typology, and then proceeds to a discussion of forms of CSB identified in the typology. The article concludes with implications of the CSB typology to practitioners and researchers interested in the consumer behavior in charitable support activities.

A TYPOLOGY OF CHARITY SUPPORT BEHAVIORS

Bendapudi, Singh, and Bendapudi (1996) developed an extensive conceptual framework and process model of helping behavior that identified three forms of helping behavior: *no help*, *token help*, and *serious help*. Although the theoretical underpinnings of this model are very well developed, the three helping behaviors are generic and provide little direction for practitioners looking for new sources of resource support. However, the Bendapudi et al. (1996) framework is particularly relevant to the current article because it offers support for the existence of high- and low-involvement supporters. Specifically, Bendapudi et al. (1996) argue that *persistent* (e.g., perceptions, motives, abilities) and *transient* (e.g., moods, media exposure, attention) donor variables serve to moderate the impact of charity promotions upon helping behavior.

Similarly, according to the decision process identified by Sargeant (1999), CSB can be exhibited by uninvolved supporters. For example, a contribution to charity can be motivated by a desire to reduce personal taxes. However, the mediating variables in the Sargeant (1999) model (i.e., fit between the organization and individual, past experience with the charity) are limited to the decision process of the involved supporter. Similarly, Bennett (2003) argued that sympathy and personal relevance of a cause are particularly important determinants of the decision to support a particular charity, again variables associated with involved supporters.

In their proposed model of brand community development, Hassay and Peloza (2004a) argue that the brand community markers of consciousness of kind (i.e., identification) and shared rituals (i.e., behavioral involvement) lead to the development of moral responsibility (i.e., perceived sense of community) and subsequently commitment to a brand or charity. Specifically, the authors suggest that consumers linked by identification with a common charitable cause increase their behavioral involvement through shared acts of support. Essentially the work of these and other researchers provide support for the current typology, one that distinguishes charity support behaviors on the basis of involvement.

The current article adopts the purchase importance view of involvement introduced by Howard and Sheth (1969). According to this conceptualization, high-involvement purchases are those important to the consumer while low-involvement purchases are unimportant (Assael, 1981). Moreover, researchers such as Assael (1981) believed that this form of involvement had a profound influence on the type of decision-making used by consumers.

In the next section, the authors expand upon the Hassay and Peloza (2004b) suggestion that involved charity supporters look for, and are willing to participate in, multiple CSB.

AN EXTENDED VIEW OF CHARITY SUPPORT

Researchers have linked volunteerism to higher levels of financial contribution (Piliavin and Chang, 1990; Schlegelmilch, Love, and Diamantopoulos, 1997; Sullivan, 2002), and charity raffle-ticket purchases (Schlegelmilch et al., 1997). Similarly, Hassay and Peloza (2004b) argued that experiential forms of charity support, such as lottery-ticket purchases, are viewed by charity supporters as incremental to rather than substitutes for other forms of support. Specifically, they proposed that experiential forms of CSB, such as charity lotteries, offer hedonic benefits unavailable through most conventional forms of CSB. The typology of CSB in Figure 1 is based on the premise that both new and existing supporters can be encouraged to offer their support or increase their existing levels of support if and when new, value-added support opportunities are made available to them.

Basil (1998) found that while financial contributions and volunteerism were related, cause-related purchasing was not related to other forms of CSB. However, her measures focused on CSB in general, rather than CSB directed toward a specific charity. Therefore, Basil's (1998) findings do not preclude the existence of a specific set of CSB for highly involved supporters since cause-related purchasing is a support activity that can

FIGURE 1. A Proposed Typology of Charity Support Behavior

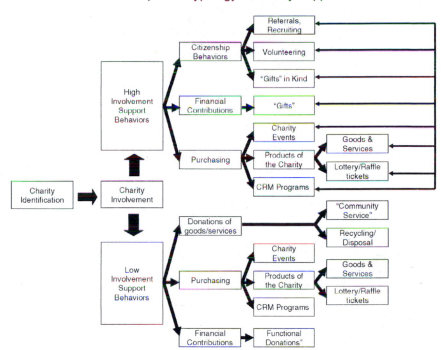

be performed by anyone and even by those completely unaware of the charity and/or its involvement.

Consequently, the typology of CSBs introduced in Figure 1 argues that although high-involvement supporters willingly and knowingly engage in multiple CSB on behalf of the charities that they support (i.e., the recursive arrows in Figure 1), the same is not true for low-involvement supporters. Further, while low-involvement supporters will engage in CSB, they have different perceptions of their support (e.g., utilitarian donations versus gifts), and are, at least initially, unlikely to purposefully engage in multiple CSB. For instance, a person may participate in a fun run or attend a charity bingo without even knowing what charity was being supported (Higgins and Lauzon, 2003). However, it is our belief that these non-traditional, less involved forms of CSB can serve as important introductions to the charity; providing the charity with an opportunity to introduce its mission and its support needs to an untapped market of neophyte supporters. And ultimately, it is believed that this introduction can lead to increased involvement and subsequent support. The various forms of CSB for involved and uninvolved supporters are discussed in greater detail in the sections that follow.

Citizenship Behaviors

Citizenship behaviors are defined as those behaviors that involve the giving of one's time and energy toward a specific charitable organization. For supporters with high involvement, these behaviors can take the form of volunteering, referrals, and gifts-in-kind. However, those who lack involvement may still perform citizenship behaviors on behalf of charity in the form of mandatory community service.

Volunteering. Similar to financial contributions, volunteerism has received extensive attention from researchers (Wilson, 2000). And as with financial contributions, many charities view volunteerism as critical to their ability to perform their missions (Wymer and Starnes, 2001). In fact, volunteerism rivals the value of individual donations, with an estimated $225 billion in labor value donated to charities in the United States in 1998 (Wymer and Starnes, 2001).

Volunteerism is a form of helping behavior that typically results from increased levels of involvement within supporters. Specifically, volunteerism is a form of planned helping that "calls for considerably more planning, sorting out of priorities, and matching of personal capabilities and interests with type of intervention" (Benson et al., 1980, 89). Affiliation with the charity or cause has been shown to be a primary predictor of volunteerism (Clary et al., 1998), and commitment is enhanced when the cause is personally relevant to the volunteer (Smith, 1980). Fisher and Ackerman (1998) argued that the decision to volunteer represents an important, even "life-altering" commitment.

Community Service. In some cases volunteer-type behaviors are performed by individuals who have little if any identification or involvement with a charity. The current article labels such quasi-volunteer acts as community service in recognition of the fact that these behaviors are rarely voluntary, but rather are forced through a legal requirement either in exchange for public goods and services or criminal punishment. In this scenario, an individual does not offer his or her services, but rather is assigned to a specific charity with which the individual may have no involvement. For example, Parsons (2002) indicated that charity retailers in the UK, in response to volunteer shortages, have had to look beyond the traditional volunteer pool to younger volunteers–those on *community service orders* and government rehabilitation/training programs, and even to paid employees. In addition, community service captures those volunteer activities that are self-serving and that are dictated by social and or employment contracts. For instance, employees may be required to participate in certain volunteer activities in order to enhance the profile of either the firm, or the career of that particular individual.

Referrals and Recruiting. Referring other supporters to the charity and recruiting new volunteers are examples of citizenship behavior. For example, prosocial behavior has been shown to increase when solicited by someone from within an individual's social network (Bendapudi et al., 1996), and the ability to socialize with friends has been shown to be a motivator of volunteer work (Broadbridge and Horne, 1994). Additionally, supporters of a charity will often recruit other members to get involved in cause-related fitness events, such as charity fun runs (Scott and Soloman, 2003).

Gifts-in-Kind. These types of gifts differ from financial contributions in that they involve the donation of either time or goods such as clothing or other personal resources. The most common form of gifts-in-kind is the one made by professionals who donate their time to the charity. The most notable examples include professional services such as legal or accounting services. Farmer and Fedor (2001) found that consistency between the charitable organizations' mission and personal values predicted the amount of time professionals spend volunteering their services to that charity.

For many charities, such gifts can have value equal to financial contributions. For example, Parsons (2002) revealed that charity retailers in the UK suffering stock shortages are actively soliciting and competing for donations of clothing and other goods from consumers.

Recycling/Disposal. In contrast to the high-involvement gifts-in-kind, individuals low in charity involvement may still donate their unwanted goods to charity. However, donations of this kind are often viewed as a way of recycling or getting rid of goods that are no longer needed; for these individuals the specific charity is relatively inconsequential. In fact, Parsons (2002) argued that charity shops have become a significant intermediary in the recycling process, with these shops acting as an entry point for a much larger series of flows for unwanted goods.

Financial Contributions

Financial contributions are defined as monetary donations made to charity. With an estimated $200 billion donated to charities in the United

States alone in 2000 (Lindahl and Conley, 2002), it is not surprising that financial contributions are the most widely researched type of CSB (e.g., Guy and Patton, 1988; Hibbert and Horne, 1996; Schlegelmilch et al., 1997).

The CSB typology illustrates that the decision to make a financial contribution to a charity is influenced by donor involvement with the charity or cause. For example, while Supphellen and Nelson (2001) indicated that recognition of the organization's name is often sufficient to generate donations from some, others give simply to "get rid of the asker" (Hibbert and Horne, 1996). To this end, it will be shown that motives for monetary donations found in the literature support our categorization of financial contributions as either functional donations or gifts-donations made by those more highly involved with a charity.

Functional Donations. Financial contributions made by those with no or little involvement in a charity are associated with the functional utility offered by such donations. For example, tax deductions have been found to be significant motivators for some donors (Dawson, 1988). Guilt has also been identified in a number of donor typologies (Guy and Patton, 1988; Sargeant, 1999). For those individuals motivated by the functional value of a monetary contribution, the specific charity is irrelevant–the benefit is gained by donating to *any* charitable organization. And according to Supphellen and Nelson (2001), in many cases donors do not evaluate or even recognize the organization or the cause.

Other motivators may be specific to a particular charity but may not require donor involvement with that charity. For example, Amos (1982) identified "condition of employment" as a motivator for financial contributions. In this scenario, a contribution is made to a specific charity, but donor involvement may be nonexistent. Similarly, forward reciprocity–essentially buying insurance against the donor needing the services of the charity at a later date–has been identified as a motivator for financial contribution (Dawson, 1988; Guy and Patton, 1988). In this scenario the donor–driven by fear (Sargeant, 1999)–need not be involved with the cause. Finally, social pressures are significant motivators of financial contributions (Amos, 1982; Guy and Patton, 1988; Smith, 1980), and although these pressures may be toward a specific charity, the individual donor may lack personal involvement with that charity.

Gifts. The difference between functional donations and gifts, then, is the degree of donor involvement with the specific charity or cause. Indeed, donation may depend on congruence between the individual and an organization's identities (Bhattacharya, Rao, and Glynn, 1995).

Although a high-involvement financial contribution may be, in part, motivated by the same egoistic rewards as functional donations, the specific charity is chosen as a result of donor involvement. In fact, Smith (1980) demonstrated that charities marked by higher involvement, such as those affiliated with religions, are able to maintain higher donation levels than other charities in the face of reduced tax advantages.

Examples of financial contributions that benefit from donor involvement include those motivated by *backward reciprocity*, where the donor is paying back services received by the charity (Dawson, 1988; Smith, 1980). Such donations are likely to benefit from existing involvement with the charity or cause. Similarly, Bennett (2003) identified "empathetic inclination" as a determinant of financial contributions, where the donor is motivated to help as a result of empathy toward a specific victim or cause.

Perceived risk is also a factor affecting donor involvement and financial contributions. Hibbert and Horne (1996) argued that the level of risk and commitment involved in the financial contribution will be positively related to donor involvement. Therefore, donor involvement at a charity collection box on the street in characterized by low risk, low commitment and therefore low involvement. Similarly, Rosenblatt, Cusson and McGown (1986) propose a relationship between perceived risk and involvement.

Finally, Batson (1994) highlighted principlism as a motive for acting in the public good. In this scenario, the support is given in order to uphold one's principles, and therefore likely to be made to a charity where the donor has existing involvement.

Purchasing

According to Barone, Miyazaki, and Taylor (2000) identification with a cause extends to the type of products that supporters buy; with consumers found to actively search for and purchase products that support causes that they identify with. Similarly, Sen and Bhattacharya (2001) found that consumers select products based on charity affiliation and are willing to pay more for products affiliated with personally relevant charities. Conversely, shoppers will boycott or disidentify with a brand because of its charity affiliations (Webb and Mohr, 1998). Webb and Mohr (1998) argued that segments of the population invest time and effort, as well as money, to develop informed responses to corporate cause-related marketing initiatives.

Consequently, identification underscores the notion that people who support a cause do not necessarily identify with it, although those who identify with a cause will support it (Bhattacharya et al., 1995). Furthermore, identification extends beyond the consumption of products sold by the charity to the products and services of third parties through cause-related marketing (CRM). In fact, according to Bennett and Gabriel (2000), these purchases provide supporters with a more visible, symbolic statement about their identification with the organization and/or cause, purchases often used as *badges* that allow supporters to define themselves in public.

Although CRM has become a widely researched form of CSB, Hassay and Peloza (2004b) emphasized that charity purchasing embodies much more than just CRM. Specifically, in the current context, charity purchasing is defined as any consumer-oriented, value-driven exchange in which the purchase of a product or service directly or indirectly generates financial returns for a charitable organization.

Event Attendance/Participation. Examples of charity events include a wide range of activities including bingos, concerts, dinners, fashion shows, and cause-related fitness events (e.g., fun runs). Despite their prevalence, there is little research on consumer behavior issues related to these events. In part, this paucity of research is explained by the fact that these events are relatively new (Scott and Solomon, 2003). Although relatively unexplored, Higgins and Lauzon (2003) illustrated that these forms of fund-raising are not inconsequential, with 15% of the $5 billion donated by Canadians to charities in 2000 tied to the sponsorship of someone in a fund-raising event. Furthermore, it has been reported that Americans spent an estimated $10 billion on more than 75,000 charity-sponsored bingo and casino games in 1993 (Johnston, 1993).

According to Gagnard (1989), charity events are the most popular form of fund-raising–a finding that Higgins and Lauzon (2003) argued is partially explained by the resemblance of these events to traditional market exchanges. Moreover, value-added fund-raising products, and especially those that offered some form of hedonic value, are likely to be well received by both current and new supporters (Cheary, 1997; Hassay and Peloza, 2004b). What distinguishes high- and low-involvement participation in charity events then is likely to be the motivation for participation. Specifically, it is believed that the charity or cause will be first and foremost in the minds of those highly involved, whereas those less involved will be focused on the leisure, entertainment, and social-networking aspects of these types of events. For example, Higgins and Lauzon (2003) found that participants of a charity fun run were either *cause-* or *event*-focused. These authors found that while this latter group of participants was aware of a charity-connection, they were unable to recall which charity or cause was involved. Scott and Solomon (2003) reported similar findings in an investigation of cause-related events.

Charity Products–Goods/Services. Although a large number of charities make and/or distribute merchandise and services for sale to consumers, there has been very little research conducted on consumer desire for and attitudes toward such products. Rather, the few articles in this area have focused on the supply side of such products, and specifically on issues of charity retailing and on charity branding and opportunities to extend the charity brand.

According to Ford and Mottner (2003), research on charity retailing is almost entirely based upon UK charity shops. In addition, Parsons (2002) reported that charity trading has grown rapidly since the 1980s, with over 6,000 charity shops operating in the U.K. combining for more £400 million in sales. And while this sales performance represents less than 1% of UK retail sales (Benady, 1997), charity retailers are experiencing growth rates that are well above those being experienced by the retail sector. Further, the list of charity products is growing into non-traditional areas such as music and whiskey (Cheary, 1997). With respect to services, the charity car wash has been a fixture in North America for years, and charities are now offering equity plans, savings and other financial services, and even adventure holidays (Bennett and Gabriel, 2000).

Moreover, a number of researchers have suggested that charity retailing is evolving from its traditional position as a purveyor of second-hand goods to mainstream retailers focused on the sale of new merchandise. This new breed of charity retailer often targets a more affluent consumer base (Parsons, 2002), many of whom are simply looking for a way to support the charity (Horne and Broadbridge, 1995).

The lack of research beyond charity retailing is surprising when one considers that the Boy Scouts of America have had exclusive rights to the name and associated logo in order to protect their right to sell merchandise in support of scouting since 1916 (Jabe, 1998), while their sister organization–the Girl Guides of Canada–have been selling private-label Girl Guide cookies as a fund-raising activity for more than 75 years.

Similar to the dichotomy of charity-event participants, it is believed that consumers will choose to purchase charity goods and services because of either product involvement (i.e., the product itself), or cause involvement.

Charity Products–Lottery/Raffle Tickets. The authors follow the Hassay and Peloza (2004b) categorization scheme and distinguish lottery/raffle-ticket purchases from not only more conventional goods and services, but also other forms of charity gaming identified previously as "charity events." The reason for assigning these charity gaming products a unique category is that they may or may not be produced by the charity (i.e., may be state-sponsored), moreover the charity may or may not be an identifiable recipient of the lottery/raffle. As with the other forms of charity purchasing, there is very little research on charity lotteries, with Peloza and Hassay (2004) a notable exception. And yet, despite this paucity of research, such lotteries have considerable appeal. In fact, North Americans spend liberally on gambling products that support charities. For example, in 1995 charities in North America raised more than $1.3 billion through gaming activities, and it has been estimated that charity gaming accounts for over 3% of total gambling revenues in the United States (*Nonprofit World,* 1996).

Again, high- and low-involvement consumers are believed to be distinguished by their purchasing motives: either to win a desirable prize or because of improved odds of winning, or out of a desire to support the focal charity. To this end, a preliminary study conducted by Peloza and Hassay (2004) revealed that a particular kind of charity lottery product, the premium-priced "charity super lottery," was more likely to be purchased by high-involvement charity supporters than low-involvement consumers.

Cause-Related Marketing. By far the most widely researched form of charity purchasing is CRM, where companies donate a portion of sales to a defined charity (Varadarajan and Menon, 1998). CRM programs have been touted as an effective source of differentiation for companies looking to distinguish their brands from their competition (Meyer, 1999; Shell, 1989). However, Chaney and Dolli (2001) found that consumers were more likely to recall the name of the charity recipient rather than the CRM sponsor firm, suggesting that the nonprofit sector benefits from such collaborations beyond the immediate financial gain. Particularly important to the current article was the Chaney and Dolli (2001) discovery that CRM is a complementary rather than substitutive form of fund-raising in the minds of consumers. Consumers in the Chaney and Dolli (2001) study also reported purchasing more of and switching to those brands associated with CRM programs.

With respect to involvement it is believed that highly involved supporters of a charity will seek out, and possibly switch, to those organizational products that support their particular cause or charity. In contrast, low-involvement consumers will simply purchase the products that offer the most value, and for some of these consumers, a CRM product may be seen as offering more value simply because it has a charity affiliation. In fact, it has been found that consumers not only exhibit a preference for companies and products that support social causes (Mohr, Webb, and Harris, 2001), but that they are also willing to pay higher prices for such products (Meyer, 1999; Webb and Mohr, 1998).

DISCUSSION AND CONCLUSION

The proposed CSB typology provides an integration of what were previously treated as primarily independent forms of support behavior, such as financial contributions and volunteerism. In addition, the proposed typology expands the current range of CSB discussed in the literature to include emerging and novel forms of CSB such as charity lotteries and the purchase of charity goods and services.

The typology highlights an important yet largely ignored segment of uninvolved charity supporters. Although most research tends to assume an audience of involved supporters (i.e., those who are passionate about a specific charity), the proposed typology suggests that uninvolved supporters may represent an important opportunity for charities, and that charities should develop support vehicles to attract uninvolved supporters. For instance, through nontraditional forms of CSB, uninvolved consumers may prove to be a significant source of financial support to a charity. More importantly, it is suggested that these nontraditional forms of support can serve as an introduction to the charity or cause that may lead to future involvement and future support.

Although it is unlikely that an initially uninvolved supporter will immediately offer allegiance to the charity, the proposed typology provides insight into strategies for charities to develop involvement in consumers. Specifically, the hierarchy-of-effects framework may be useful in providing an opportunity for charities to leverage initial contacts with uninvolved consumers to develop long-term involved supporters. These initial contacts represent opportunities for charities to communicate their mission or impress upon the consumer the importance or severity of their cause. Such awareness, and subsequent attitudes and intentions, are often used to assess impact in hierarchical conceptualizations of the communications process (e.g., McGuire, 1976).

However, not all uninvolved consumers represent potential donors. The consumption motive arguably remains the most significant determinant for both initial and continued purchase of charity-supported goods and/or services. For example, products are often purchased and consumed without awareness that these products support a charity. In this case, the motive may be utilitarian (e.g., a useful product at an attractive price), or hedonic (as may be the case with charity gaming). In fact, many purchases are made with only limited decision-making effort, and therefore little or no consideration for the charitable cause is given. This again underscores how important it is for charities to ensure that their message is delivered and reinforced through all communication vehicles, and that consumers are exposed to their purpose or need.

The involvement segmentation provides charity marketers with an important opportunity to increase consumer support and commitment. To this end, charities should consider creating additional CSB opportunities for highly involved supporters. For example, novel support opportunities such as charity lotteries have been shown to generate incremental support to existing fund-raising and volunteer efforts. In fact, the proposed typology represents an important step in developing an integrated view of CSB, one that allows charities to maximize support from involved consumers. Further, involved supporters should be targeted when charities develop what are traditionally considered uninvolved forms of support, such as charity gaming, as these novel support products likely tap what were heretofore untapped consumption values (Hassay and Peloza, 2004b).

Finally, the current article highlights a number of future research opportunities. First, research is needed to better understand the different consumption values sought and received by involved consumers who engage in multiple CSB. For example, does a CSB such as charity gaming indeed complement other forms such as volunteering, or does one replace the other? Second, more study is needed into the decision-making process of consumers who move from uninvolved to involved supporters. Research might, for instance, explore how best to introduce uninvolved consumers to the charity mission or need. Another important question to be answered is, To what degree does the form of initial contact (e.g., hedonic versus altruistic) affect consumer attitudes toward the organization and the decision to become more involved? Lastly, future research should examine how to leverage existing "brand" communities (Muniz and O'Guinn, 2001) within the charity sector to attract new supporters, and develop and maintain long-term relationships with existing supporters.

REFERENCES

Amos, Orley (1982), "Empirical Analysis of Motives Underlying Individual Contributions to Charity," *Atlantic Economic Journal, 1*(4), 45-52.

Assael, Henry (1981), *Consumer Behavior and Executive Action*, Boston: Kent.

Barone, Michael, Anthony Miyazaki, and Kimberly Taylor (2000), "The Influence of Cause-Related Marketing on Consumer Choice: Does One Good Turn Deserve Another?" *Academy of Marketing Science Journal, 28*(2), 248–62.

Basil, Debra Z. (1998), "Three Faces of Charity: Donations, Volunteerism, and Cause-Related Purchases," Working Paper Session in *Advances in Consumer Research*, Vol. 25, ed. Joseph W. Alba and J. Wesley Hutchinson, Provo, UT: Association for Consumer Research, 75-86.

Batson, Daniel (1994), "Why Act For the Public Good? Four Answers," *Personality and Social Psychology Bulletin, 20*(5), 603-10.

Benady, David (1995), "Charity Shops Adapt to Survive," *Marketing Week, 20*(12), 36-7.

Bendapudi, Neeli, Surendra Singh, and Venkat Bendapudi (1996), "Enhancing Helping Behavior: An Integrative Framework for Promotion Planning," *Journal of Marketing, 60*(July), 33-49.

Bennett, Roger (2003), "Factors Underlying the Inclination to Donate to Particular Charity Types," *International Journal of Nonprofit and Voluntary Sector Marketing, 8*(1), 12-29.

Bennett, Roger and Helen Gabriel (2000), "Charity Affiliation as a Determinant of Product Purchase Decisions," *Journal of Product and Brand Management, 9*(4), 255-70.

Benson, P., J. Dehority, L. Garman, E. Hanson, M. Hochschwender, C. Lebold, R. Rohr, and J. Sullivan (1980), "Intrapersonal Correlates of Nonspontaneous Helping Behavior," *Journal of Social Psychology, 110*, 87-95.

Bhattacharya, C.B., Hayagreeva Rao, and Mary Ann Glynn (1995), "Understanding the Bond of Identification: An Investigation of its Correlates Among Art Museum Members, *Journal of Marketing, 59*(4), 46-68.

Broadbridge, Adelina and Suzanne Horne (1994), "Who Volunteers for Charity Retailing and Why," *The Services Industries Journal*, 14 (4), 421-37.

Bussell, Helen and Deborah Forbes (2002), "Understanding the Volunteer Market: The What, Where, Who and Why of Volunteering," *International Journal of Nonprofit and Voluntary Sector Marketing*," 7(3), 244–57.

Chaney, Isabella and Nitha Dolli (2001), "Cause Related Marketing in New Zealand," *International Journal of Nonprofit and Voluntary Sector Marketing, 6*(2), 156-63.

Cheary, Natalie (1997), "Charities Try Branded Goods to Beat Slump," *Marketing Week, 20*(14), 24.

Clary, E. Gil, Robert Ridge, Arthur Stukas, Mark Snyder, John Copeland, Julie Haugen, and Peter Miene (1998), "Understanding and Assessing the Motivations of Volunteers: A Functional Approach," *Journal of Personality and Social Psychology, 74*(6), 1516-30.

Dawson, Scott (1988), "Four Motivations for Charitable Giving: Implications for Marketing Strategy to Attract Donations for Medical Research," *Journal of Health Care Marketing, 8*(2), 31-37.

Farmer, Steven and Donald Fedor (2001), "Changing the Focus on Volunteering: An Investigation of Volunteers' Multiple Contributions to a Charitable Organization," *Journal of Management, 27*, 191-211.

Fisher, Robert and David Ackerman (1998), "The Effects of Recognition and Group Need on Volunteerism: A Social Norm Perspective," *Journal of Consumer Research, 25*, 262–75.

Ford, John B. and Sandra Mottner (2003), "Retailing in the Nonprofit Sector: An Exploratory Analysis of Church-Connected Retailing Ventures," *International Journal of Nonprofit and Voluntary Sector Marketing, 8*(3), 337-48.

Gagnard, A., (1989), "Community Study Suggests Segmentation Strategies," *Journal of Volunteer Administration, 7*(Summer), 14-18.

Guy, Bonnie and Wesley Patton (1988), "The Marketing of Altruistic Causes: Understanding Why People Help," *Journal of Services Marketing, 2*(1), 5-16.

Hassay, Derek N. and John Peloza (2004a), "Extending the Concept of Brand Community: Building Commitment in the Charity Sector," working paper, Haskayne School of Business, Calgary, Alberta.

Hassay, Derek N. and John Peloza (2004b), "*FUN*draising: Having Fun While Raising Funds," *Advances in Consumer Research*, forthcoming.

Hibbert, Sally and Suzanne Horne (1996), "Giving To Charity: Questioning the Donor Process," *Journal of Consumer Marketing, 13*(2), 4-11.

Higgins, Joan Wharf and Lara Lauzon (2003), "Finding the Funds in Fun Runs," *International Journal of Nonprofit and Voluntary Sector Marketing, 8*(4), 363-77.

Horne, Suzanne and Adelina Broadbridge (1995), "Charity Shops: A Classification by Merchandise Mix," *International Journal of Retail and Distribution Management, 23*(7), 17-23.

Howard, John A. and Jagdish N. Sheth (1969), *The Theory of Buyer Behavior*, New York: John Wiley and Sons.

Jabe, Daniel N. (1998), "The Sons of the Nation: The Popular Appeal of the Boy Scouts of America, 1910-1919," unpublished thesis submitted to the History Department of the University of Michigan.

Johnston, David (1993), "The Dark Side of Charity Gambling," *Money, 22*(10), 130–35.

Liao, Mei-Na, Susan Foreman, and Adrian Sargeant (2001), "Market Versus Societal Orientation in the Nonprofit Context," *International Journal of Nonprofit and Voluntary Sector Marketing, 6*(3), 254–68.

Lindahl, Wesley and Aaron Conley (2002), "Literature Review: Philanthropic Fundraising," *Nonprofit Management and Leadership, 13*(1), 91–112.

McGuire, William J. (1976), "Some Internal Psychological Factors Influencing Consumer Choice," *Journal of Consumer Research, 2*(4), 302-19.

Meyer, Harvey (1999), "When the Cause is Just," *The Journal of Business Strategy, 20*(6), 27-31.

Mohr, Lois, Deborah Webb, and Katherine Harris (2001), "Do Consumers Expect Companies to be Socially Responsible? The Impact of Corporate Social Responsibility on Buying Behavior," *Journal of Consumer Affairs, 35*(1), 45-72.

Muniz, Albert Jr. and Thomas O'Guinn (2001), "Brand Community," *Journal of Consumer Research, 27*(4), 412–32.

Nonprofit World (1996), "Charities Turning to Gaming Fundraisers," 14 (6), 9.

Parsons, Elizabeth (2002), "Charity Retail: Past, Present and Future," *International Journal of Retail and Distribution Management, 23*(7), 17-23.

Peloza, John and Derek N. Hassay (2004), "When Vice Makes Nice: The Viability and Virtuousness of Charity Lotteries," *Proceedings of the Marketing and Public Policy Conference*, Vol. 14, ed. D. Scammon, M. Mason, and R. Mayer, Chicago, IL: AMA, 156-59.

Piliavin, Jane and Hong-Wen Chang (1990), "Altruism: A Review of Recent Theory and Research," *Annual Review of Sociology, 16*, 27-65.

Rosenblatt, Jerry, Alain Cusson, and Lee McGown (1986), "A Model to Explain Charitable Donation–Health Case Consumer Behavior," in *Advances in Consumer Research*, Vol. 13, ed., Richard Lutz, Provo, UT: Association for Consumer Research, 235-39.

Sargeant, Adrian (1999), "Charitable Giving: Towards a Model of Donor Behavior," *Journal of Marketing Management, 15*(4), 215-38.

Schlegelmilch, Bodo, Alix Love, and Adamantios Diamantopoulos (1997), "Responses to Different Charity Appeals: The Impact of Donor Characteristics on the Amount of Donations," *European Journal of Marketing, 31*(8), 548-60.

Scott, Andrea and Paul Solomon (2003), "The Marketing of Cause-Related Events: A Study of Participants as Consumers," *Journal of Nonprofit and Public Sector Marketing, 11*(2), 43-66.

Sen, Sankar and C.B. Bhattacharya (2001), "Does Doing Good Always Lead to Doing Better? Consumer Reactions to Corporate Social Responsibility," *Journal of Marketing Research, 38*(2), 225-43.

Shell, Adam (1989), "Cause-Related Marketing: Big Risks, Big Potential," *Public Relations Journal, 45*(7), 8-9.

Smith, Scott (1980), "Giving to Charitable Organizations: A Behavioral Review and a Framework for Increasing Commitment," in *Advances in Consumer Research*, Vol. 7, ed. Jerry Olson, Provo, UT: Association for Consumer Research, 753-56.

Sullivan, Aline (2002), "Affair of the Heart," *Barron's, 82*(49), 28.

Supphellen, Magne and Michelle Nelson (2001), "Developing, Exploring and Validating A Typology of Private Philanthropic Decision Making," *Journal of Economic Psychology, 22*(5), 573-603.

Varadarajan, Rajan and Anil Menon (1988), "Cause-Related Marketing: A Coalignment of Marketing Strategy and Corporate Philanthropy," *Journal of Marketing, 52*(3), 58–74.

Webb, Deborah and Lois Mohr, (1998) "A Typology of Consumer Responses to Cause-Related Marketing: From Skeptics to Socially Concerned," *Journal of Public Policy and Marketing, 17*(2), 226-38.

Williamson, Richard (2003), "Money Supply Soars, but Funding is a Different Question," *The NonProfit Times*, June 15.

Wilson, John (2000), "Volunteering," *American Review of Sociology, 26*, 215–40.

Wymer, Walter and Becky Starnes (2001), "Conceptual Foundations and Practical Guidelines for Recruiting Volunteers to Serve in Local Nonprofit Organizations: Part I," *Journal of Nonprofit and Public Sector Marketing," 9*(3), 63-95.

doi:10.1300/J054v17n01_07

Index